Principles and Standards for School Mathematics Navigations Series

NAVIGATING

through

NUMBER

and

OPERATIONS

in

GRADES 6–8

Sid Rachlin
Kathleen Cramer
Connie Finseth
Linda Cooper Foreman
Dorothy Geary
Seth Leavitt
Margaret Schwan Smith

Susan N. Friel
Grades 6–8 Editor

Peggy A. House
Navigations Series Editor

NCTM®

NATIONAL COUNCIL OF
TEACHERS OF MATHEMATICS

Copyright © 2006 by
The National Council of Teachers of Mathematics, Inc.
1906 Association Drive, Reston, VA 20191-1502
(703) 620-9840; (800) 235-7566; www.nctm.org

Library of Congress Cataloging-in-Publication Data

Navigating through number and operations in grades 6-8 / Sid Rachlin ...
[et al.] ; Susan N. Friel, grades 6-8 editor.
    p. cm. -- (Principles and standards for school mathematics
navigations series)
 Includes bibliographical references.
 ISBN 0-87353-575-8
 1. Mathematics--Study and teaching (Middle school)--United States. 2.
Mathematics--Study and teaching (Middle school)--Activity programs. 3.
Numeration--Study and teaching (Middle school) 4. Numerical
calculations--Study and teaching (Middle school) 5. Problem solving in
children. 6. Reasoning in children. I. Rachlin, Sid. II. Friel, Susan N.
III. National Council of Teachers of Mathematics. IV. Series.
 QA13N385 2005
 510.71'2--dc22
                                                              2005027287

The National Council of Teachers of Mathematics is a public voice of mathematics education, providing vision, leadership, and professional development to support teachers in ensuring mathematics learning of the highest quality for all students.

Printed in the United States of America

NAVIGATIONS
SERIES

TABLE OF CONTENTS

CONTENTS OF THE CD-ROM

Introduction

Table of Standards and Expectations, Number and Operations, Pre-K–12

Applets

Scale 'n Pop
Fraction Four
Learning about Multiplication
Multiplication of Fractions
Adding Decimals—Circle 3

Blackline Masters

All the Blackline Masters listed above plus the following:
Linden's Algorithm—Diagrams
Linden's Algorithm Revisited—Diagrams
Timberline Track Team
Jamaal's Snowstorm
City Soccer Fields

Readings from Publications of the National Council of Teachers of Mathematics

A Complete Model for Operations on Integers
   Michael T. Battista
   Arithmetic Teacher

Problems That Encourage Proportion Sense
   Esther M. H. Billings
   Mathematics Teaching in the Middle School

Modifying Our Questions to Assess Students' Thinking
   Michaele F. Chappell and Denisse R. Thompson
   Mathematics Teaching in the Middle School

Presenting and Representing: From Fractions to Rational Numbers
   Susan J. Lamon
   The Role of Representation in School Mathematics
   2001 Yearbook of the National Council of Teachers of Mathematics

Three Balloons for Two Dollars: Developing Proportional Reasoning
   Cynthia W. Langrall and Jane Swafford
   Mathematics Teaching in the Middle School

About This Book

Mathematics curricula have always focused on helping students develop a concept of number and the ability to use numbers to solve problems. Comfort with numbers serves as the foundation for almost everything else that students do in mathematics—and for many things that they do in life. To help students build comprehension of number and operations, *Principles and Standards for School Mathematics* (National Council of Teachers of Mathematics [NCTM] 2000) outlines the skills and understanding that students should gain as they progress from prekindergarten through grade 12. During the middle grades, students must deepen their understanding of fractions, decimals, percents, and integers. Students should also gain facility with the concept of proportionality. This skill can arise naturally as students explore other important number concepts at this grade level, including ratios and rates.

This book can serve as a guide through some of these important middle-grades explorations of number and operations. Each chapter analyzes one major thread of the Number and Operations Standard and helps you and your students explore it in depth. Underlying each of the three chapters is the expectation that students in grades 6–8 will develop and refine their computational fluency on the basis of a firm conceptual foundation.

Chapter 1, "Fractions, Decimals, and Percents," includes discussion and activities designed to help you foster your students' understanding of and facility with these important rational forms. This chapter offers ideas for expanding students' previous experiences with fractions and decimals so that they can develop a meaningful understanding of rational numbers. The activities help students see how context influences which representational forms of rational numbers—fractions, decimals, or percents—might be most efficient for solving problems. The activities also help you assess and build on students' conceptual understanding of the equivalence of rational-number representations. The chapter emphasizes experiences with the following:

- Exploring fractions, decimals, and percents as contextual representations of rational numbers
- Making connections between the different representations of rational numbers and the context in which they appear
- Using visual models and applied problems to enhance understanding of rational numbers

Chapter 2, "Working with Fractions, Decimals, and Percents," delves deeper into rational numbers—the primary numerical domain of mathematics study in the middle grades. The activities foster students' conceptual understanding of and facility and fluency with rational numbers. The activities also encourage you to give your students regular opportunities to examine one another's thinking, conjectures, and generalizations about important mathematical ideas. This chapter focuses on building students' skills in the following:

- Developing computational algorithms that call on students' understanding of the four basic numerical operations

"Instructional programs from prekindergarten through grade 12 should enable all students to—

- *understand numbers, ways of representing numbers, relationships among numbers, and number systems;*

- *understand meanings of operations and how they relate to one another;*

- *compute fluently and make reasonable estimates."*

(NCTM 2000, p. 32)

- Solving applied problems by using fractions, decimals, and percents flexibly and meaningfully
- Using context—real world, numerical, or mathematical—to associate meanings with an operation or algorithm

Chapter 3, "Proportional Reasoning," focuses on extending students' understanding of the important ideas of the rational numbers and their operations. This understanding evolves naturally from problem-solving and reasoning activities that concurrently help students develop a deeper understanding of proportionality. The chapter emphasizes experiences with the following:

- Identifying the multiplicative relationship underlying all proportional contexts
- Viewing multiplicative relationships in multiple representations, such as data tables, graphs, and equations
- Developing facility with proportionality through many areas of the curriculum and by exploring many real-world phenomena

Proportionality is woven through many areas of mathematics study, and you can find more on this topic in other books in the Navigations Series. See complementary activities for developing middle-grades students' proportional reasoning in *Navigating through Data Analysis in Grades 6-8* (Bright et al. 2003) and *Navigating through Measurement in Grades 6-8* (Bright et al. 2005).

Each chapter in this book begins with a discussion of the important mathematical ideas. Then, to give you tools for exploring these ideas with your students, each chapter offers a set of related classroom activities. The first activity in each chapter helps you evaluate your students' current understanding of the concepts. The remaining activities help you guide students through the concepts, comprehending them more deeply and building new skills and understandings. Each activity includes goals, required materials, procedures, and a discussion of the ideas and the learning that should be taking place. For many activities, you will see extensive examples and discussions of the problem-solving approaches of actual students. These illustrations show how your students might approach the activities and how you can support their explorations of these concepts. This book also includes some ideas for extending learning with technology and additional activities.

Each activity has a corresponding blackline master, signaled by an icon in the margin and included in the appendix, for use with the students. Solutions appear in the appendix as well. The blackline masters can also be printed from the CD-ROM that accompanies the book. Margin notes highlight teaching tips, background notes, and related resources. Pertinent quotations from *Principles and Standards* also appear in the margin and are signaled by an icon.

Besides the print-ready versions of the blackline masters, the accompanying CD-ROM contains computer applets for students to manipulate to extend their understanding of important concepts. The CD also features related articles to support your professional development and further understanding of the mathematical learning involved in mastering the ideas explored in this book. An icon in the margin of the book signals material on the CD-ROM.

Key to Icons

Principles and Standards

CD-ROM

Blackline Master

Three different icons appear in the book, as shown in the key. One alerts readers to material quoted from *Principles and Standards for School Mathematics,* another points them to supplementary materials on the CD-ROM that accompanies the book, and a third signals the blackline masters and indicates their locations in the appendix.

As is true of the other books in the Navigations Series, the materials presented here form a collection of activities and investigations rather than a comprehensive course of study. This volume cannot address all the important areas related to number and operations in grades 6–8, notably (1) developing a conceptual understanding of and a computational facility with integers and (2) developing a conceptual understanding of irrational numbers. To incorporate explorations of these areas, you might turn to models that previously helped students learn number concepts. For instance, you can introduce your students to integer operations through the familiar tools of number lines and two-colored chips. Similarly, you can introduce them to irrational numbers through work with areas on a geoboard.

The authors hope that you will search for additional materials that can help you deepen your students' understanding of all the important mathematical ideas related to number and operations outlined in *Principles and Standards*. Among the many resources that exist, you might find helpful *Making Sense of Fractions, Ratios, and Proportions* (NCTM 2002b) and its companion booklet *Classroom Activities for "Making Sense of Fractions, Ratios, and Proportions"* (NCTM 2002a). Another helpful resource is the "Proportional Reasoning" Focus Issue of *Mathematics Teaching in the Middle School* (NCTM 2003). These materials can complement and extend the discussions of and activities for number and operations in this Navigations book.

The coauthors of this Navigations volume are teachers of grades 6–8, researchers, and curriculum developers. With their various experiences, these authors present a multifaceted perspective on exploring concepts of number and operations with students in the middle grades. Although the names have all been changed, the examples of students' work come from the classrooms of Connie Finseth, Dorothy Geary, and Seth Leavitt, the classroom teachers on the writing team.

Battista (1983; available on the CD-ROM) details a model for helping students in the middle grades apply what they know about whole-number operations to operations with integers.

"In grades 6–8, students in the middle grades should deepen their understanding of fractions, decimals, percents, and integers, and they should become proficient in using them to solve problems. By solving problems that require multiplicative comparisons (e.g., "How many times as many?" or "How many per?"), students will gain extensive experience with ratios, rates, and percents, which helps form a solid foundation for their understanding of, and facility with, proportionality." (NCTM 2000, p. 215)

NAVIGATING *through* NUMBER *and* OPERATIONS

Introduction

What could be more fundamental in mathematics than numbers and the operations that we perform with them? Thus, it is no surprise that Number and Operations heads the list of the five Content Standards in *Principles and Standards for School Mathematics* (NCTM 2000). Yet, numbers and arithmetic are so familiar to most of us that we run the risk of underestimating the deep, rich knowledge and proficiency that this Standard encompasses.

Fundamentals of an Understanding of Number and Operations

In elaborating the Number and Operations Standard, *Principles and Standards* recommends that instructional programs from prekindergarten through grade 12 enable all students to—

- understand numbers, ways of representing numbers, relationships among numbers, and number systems;
- understand meanings of operations and how they relate to one another;
- compute fluently and make reasonable estimates.

The vision that *Principles and Standards* outlines in the description of this Standard gives Number and Operations centrality across the entire mathematics curriculum. The *Navigating through Number and Operations* volumes flesh out that vision and make it concrete in activities for students in four grade bands: prekindergarten through grade 2, grades 3–5, grades 6–8, and grades 9–12.

Understanding numbers, ways of representing numbers, relationships among numbers, and number systems

Young children begin to develop primitive ideas of number even before they enter school, and they arrive in the classroom with a range of informal understanding. They have probably learned to extend the appropriate number of fingers when someone asks, "How old are you?" and their vocabulary almost certainly includes some number words. They are likely to be able to associate these words correctly with small collections of objects, and they probably have been encouraged to count things, although they may not yet have mastered the essential one-to-one matching of objects to number names. During the years from prekindergarten through grade 2, their concepts and skills related to numbers and numeration, counting, representing and comparing quantities, and the operations of adding and subtracting will grow enormously as these ideas become the focus of the mathematics curriculum.

The most important accomplishments of the primary years include the refinement of children's understanding of counting and their initial development of number sense. Multiple classroom contexts offer numerous opportunities for students to count a myriad of things, from how many children are in their reading group, to how many cartons of milk their class needs for lunch, to how many steps they must take from the chalkboard to the classroom door. With experience, they learn to establish a one-to-one matching of objects counted with number words or numerals, and in time they recognize that the last number named is also the total number of objects in the collection. They also discover that the result of the counting process is not affected by the order in which they enumerate the objects. Eventually, they learn to count by twos or fives or tens or other forms of "skip counting," which requires that quantities be grouped in certain ways.

Though children initially encounter numbers by counting collections of physical objects, they go on to develop number concepts and the ability to think about numbers without needing the actual objects before them. They realize, for example, that five is one more than four and six is one more than five, and that, in general, the next counting number is one more than the number just named, whether or not actual objects are present for them to count. Through repeated experience, they also discover some important relationships, such as the connection between a number and its double, and they explore multiple ways of representing numbers, such as modeling six as six ones, or two threes, or three twos, or one more than five, or two plus four.

Young children are capable of developing number concepts that are more sophisticated than adults sometimes expect. Consider the prekindergarten child who explained her discovery that some numbers, like 2 and 4 and 6, are "fair numbers," or "sharing numbers," because she could divide these numbers of cookies equally with a friend, but numbers like 3 or 5 or 7 are not "fair numbers," because they do not have this property.

As children work with numbers, they discover ways of thinking about the relationships among them. They learn to compare two numbers to determine which is greater. If they are comparing 17 and 20, for example, they might match objects in two collections to see that 3 objects are "left over" in the set of 20 after they have "used up" the set of 17, or they might count on from 17 and find that they have to count three more numbers to get to 20. By exploring "How many more?" and "How many less?" young children lay the foundations for addition and subtraction.

Continual work with numbers in the primary grades contributes to students' development of an essential, firm understanding of place-value concepts and the base-ten numeration system. This understanding often emerges from work with concrete models, such as base-ten blocks or linking cubes, which engage students in the process of grouping and ungrouping units and tens. They must also learn to interpret, explain, and model the meaning of two- and three-digit numbers written symbolically. By the end of second grade, *Principles and Standards* expects students to be able to count into the hundreds, discover patterns in the numeration system related to place value, and compose (create through different combinations) and decompose (break apart in different ways) two- and three-digit numbers.

In addition, students in grade 2 should begin to extend their understanding of whole numbers to include early ideas about fractions. Initial experiences with fractions should introduce simple concepts, such as the idea that halves or fourths signify divisions of things into two or four equal parts, respectively.

As students move into grades 3–5, their study of numbers expands to include larger whole numbers as well as fractions, decimals, and negative numbers. Now the emphasis shifts from addition and subtraction to multiplication and division, and the study of numbers focuses more directly on the multiplicative structure of the base-ten numeration system. Students should understand a number like 435 as representing $(4 \times 100) + (3 \times 10) + (5 \times 1)$, and they should explore what happens to numbers when they multiply or divide them by powers of 10.

The number line now becomes an important model for representing the positions of numbers in relation to benchmarks like 1/2, 1, 10, 100, 500, and so on. It also provides a useful tool at this stage for representing fractions, decimals, and negative integers as well as whole numbers.

Concepts of fractions that the curriculum treated informally in the primary grades gain new meaning in grades 3–5 as students learn to interpret fractions both as parts of a whole and as divisions of numbers. Various models contribute to students' developing understanding. For example, an area model in which a circle or a rectangle is divided into equal parts, some of which are shaded, helps students visualize fractions as parts of a unit whole or determine equivalent fractions.

Number-line models are again helpful, allowing students to compare fractions to useful benchmarks. For instance, they can decide that 3/5 is greater than 1/3 because 3/5 is more than 1/2 but 1/3 is less than 1/2,

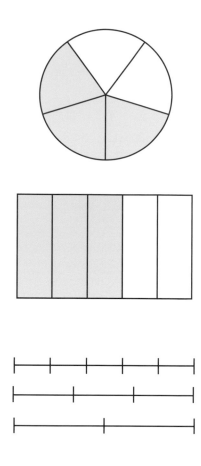

or they can recognize that 9/10 is greater than 7/8 because 9/10 is closer to 1 than 7/8 is. Parallel number lines, such as one marked in multiples of 1/3 and another in multiples of 1/6, can help students identify equivalences.

During these upper elementary years, students also encounter the concept of percent as another model for a part of a whole. Their work should help them begin to develop benchmarks for common percentages, such as 25 percent, $33\frac{1}{3}$ percent, or 50 percent.

In grades 6–8, students expand their understanding of numbers to include the integers, and now they learn how to add, subtract, multiply, and divide with negative as well as positive numbers. Developing a deeper understanding of rational numbers is another very important goal for these students, who must increase their facility in working with rational numbers represented by fractions, decimals, and percents.

At this level, the curriculum places particular emphasis on developing proportional reasoning, which requires students to understand and use ratios, proportions, and rates to model and solve problems. Fraction strips, circles, number lines, area models, hundreds grids, and other physical models provide concrete representations from which students can draw conceptual meaning as they hone their understanding of rational numbers. Exposure to these models develops students' abilities to translate fluently from one representation to another, to compare and order rational numbers, and to attach meaning to rational numbers expressed in different but equivalent forms.

The concept of proportionality, which is a central component of the middle-school curriculum, serves to connect many aspects of mathematics, such as the slope of the linear function $y = mx$ in algebra, the scale factor in measurements on maps or scale drawings, the ratio of the circumference to the diameter of a circle (π) in geometry, or the relative frequency of a statistic in a set of data. Thus, students have numerous opportunities to develop and use number concepts in multiple contexts and applications. In some of those contexts, students encounter very large or very small numbers, which necessitate scientific notation and a sense of orders of magnitude of numbers.

Finally, students in grades 6–8 are able to focus more directly on properties of numbers than they were at earlier stages of development. They can investigate such key ideas as the notions of factor and multiple, prime and composite numbers, factor trees, divisibility tests, special sets (like the triangular and square numbers), and many interesting number patterns and relationships, including an introduction to some irrational numbers, such as $\sqrt{2}$.

When students move on to grades 9–12, their understanding of number should continue to grow and mature. In these grades, students customarily encounter many problems, both in mathematics and in related disciplines like science or economics, where very large and very small numbers are commonplace. In working such problems, students can use technology that displays large and small numbers in several ways, such as 1.219 E17 for 1.219 (10^{17}), and they need to become fluent in expressing and interpreting such quantities.

High school students also have many opportunities to work with irrational numbers, and these experiences should lead them to an understanding of the real number system—and, beyond that, to an understanding of number systems themselves. Moreover, students in grades 9–12 should develop an awareness of the relationship of those systems to various types of equations. For example, they should understand that the equation $A + 5 = 10$ has a whole-number solution, but the equation $A + 10 = 5$ does not, though it does have an integer solution. They should recognize that the equation $10 \cdot A = 5$ requires the rational numbers for its solution, and the equation $A^2 = 5$ has a real-number solution, but the equation $A^2 + 10 = 5$ is solved in the complex numbers.

Students should also understand the one-to-one correspondence between real numbers and points on the number line. They should recognize important properties of real numbers, such as that between any two real numbers there is always another real number, or that irrational numbers can be only approximated, but never represented exactly, by fractions or repeating decimals.

In grades 9–12, students also encounter new systems, such as vectors and matrices, which they should explore and compare to the more familiar number systems. Such study will involve them in explicit examination of the associative, commutative, and distributive properties and will expand their horizons to include a system (matrices) in which multiplication is not commutative. Using matrices, students can represent and solve a variety of problems in other areas of mathematics. They can find solutions to systems of linear equations, for instance, or describe a transformation of a geometric figure in the plane. Using algebraic symbols and reasoning, students also can explore interesting number properties and relationships, determining, for example, that the sum of two consecutive triangular numbers is always a square number and that the sum of the first N consecutive odd integers is equal to N^2.

Understanding meanings of operations and how operations relate to one another

As young children in prekindergarten through grade 2 learn to count and develop number sense, they simultaneously build their understanding of addition and subtraction. This occurs naturally as children compare numbers to see who collected more stickers or as they solve problems like the following: "When Tim and his dad went fishing, they caught seven fish. Tim caught four of the fish. How many did his dad catch?" Often, children use concrete materials, such as cubes or chips, to model "joining" or "take-away" problems, and they develop "counting on" or "counting back" strategies to solve problems about "how many altogether?" and "how many more?" and similar relationships.

Even at this early stage, teachers who present problems in everyday contexts can represent the problem symbolically. For example, teachers can represent the problem "How many more books does Emily need to read if she has already read 13 books and wants to read 20 books before the end of the school year?" as $13 + \square = 20$ or as $20 - \square = 13$. Such expressions help students to see the relationship between addition and subtraction.

Young children also build an understanding of the operations when they explain the thinking behind their solutions. For example, a child who had just celebrated his sixth birthday wondered, "How much is

6 and 7?" After thinking about the problem for a moment, he decided that 6 + 7 = 13, and then he explained how he knew: "Well, I just had a birthday, and for my birthday I got two 'five dollars,' and my $5 and $5 are $10, so 6 and 6 should be 12, and then 6 and 7 must be 13."

As young students work with addition and subtraction, they should also be introduced to the associative and commutative properties of the operations. They should learn that when they are doing addition, they can use the numbers in any order, but they should discover that this fact is not true for subtraction. Further, they should use the commutative property to develop effective strategies for computation. For example, they might rearrange the problem 3 + 5 + 7 to 3 + 7 + 5 = (3 + 7) + 5 = 10 + 5 = 15.

Early work with addition and subtraction also lays the conceptual groundwork for later study of operations. Multiplication and division are all but evident when students repeatedly add the same number—for example, in skip-counting by twos or fives—or when they solve problems requiring that a collection of objects be shared equally among several friends. The strategies that young children use to solve such problems, either repeatedly adding the same number or partitioning a set into equal-sized subsets, later mature into computational strategies for multiplication and division.

The operations of multiplication and division, and the relationships between them, receive particular emphasis in grades 3–5. Diagrams, pictures, and concrete manipulatives play important roles as students deepen their understanding of these operations and develop their facility in performing them.

For example, if an area model calls for students to arrange 18 square tiles into as many different rectangles as they can, the students can relate the three possible solutions (1 by 18, 2 by 9, and 3 by 6) to the factors of 18. Similar problems will show that some numbers, like 36 or 64, have many possible rectangular arrangements and hence many factors, while other numbers, like 37 or 41, yield only one solution and thus have only two factors. By comparing pairs of rectangular arrangements, such as 3 by 6 and 6 by 3, students can explore the commutative property for multiplication. As illustrated in the three examples below,

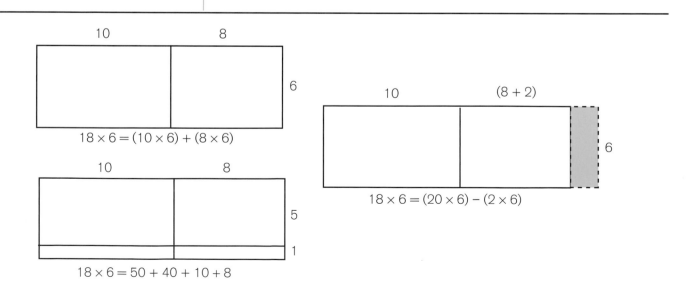

by decomposing an 18-by-6 area model, students can develop an understanding of the distributive property.

Other models for multiplication might involve rates or combinations. In grades 3–5, a typical problem involving a rate might be, "If 4 pencils cost 69¢, how much will a dozen pencils cost?" Problems involving combinations at this level are often similar to the following: "How many different kinds of meat-and-cheese sandwiches can we make if we have 2 kinds of bread (white and wheat), 4 kinds of meat (beef, ham, chicken, and turkey), and 3 kinds of cheese (Swiss, American, and provolone)?" (See the tree diagram below.)

To develop students' understanding of division, teachers should engage them in working with two different models—a partitioning model ("If you have 36 marbles and want to share them equally among 4 people, how many marbles should each person receive?") and a repeated-subtraction model ("If you have 36 marbles and need to place 4 marbles into each cup in a game, how many cups will you fill?"). Students should be able to represent both models with manipulatives and diagrams.

In exploring division, students in grades 3–5 will inevitably encounter situations that produce a remainder, and they should examine what the remainder means, how large it can be for a given divisor, and how to interpret it in different contexts. For example, arithmetically,

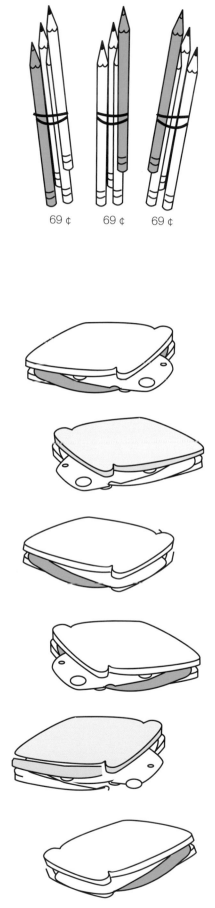

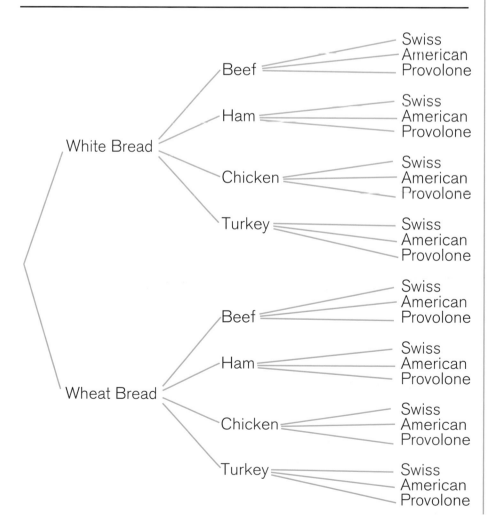

$28 \div 5 = 5\frac{3}{5}$, but consider the solutions to each of the following problems:

- "Compact disks are on sale for $28 for 5 disks. How much should one disk cost?" ($5.60)
- "Muffins are packaged 5 to a box for the bake sale. How many boxes can you make up if you bake 28 muffins?" (5).
- "Parents will be transporting children in minivans for the class field trip. Each van can take 5 children. The class has 28 children. How many vans will parents need to drive for the trip?" (6).

The understanding of all four operations that students build with whole numbers in the upper elementary grades broadens during grades 6–8, when they apply those operations to fractions, decimals, percents, and integers. Moreover, as students operate with rational numbers and integers, they encounter new contexts that may challenge their conceptual foundations. For example, when students are multiplying or dividing with fractions or decimals between 0 and 1, they see results that expose as misconceptions the commonly held beliefs that "multiplication makes larger" and "division makes smaller."

Other challenges that middle-grades students must confront include understanding when the result of a computation with integers is positive and when it is negative, knowing how to align decimals in computations with decimal fractions, and recognizing where in an answer to place a decimal point. Operating with fractions has proven difficult for many students. Lacking conceptual understanding, many have tried to get by with rote application of procedures that they don't understand. In the middle grades, therefore, it is important that students develop an understanding of the meaning of such concepts as numerator, denominator, and equivalent fractions and their roles in adding and subtracting fractions.

Middle school students need to model and compare expressions that are frequently subject to confusion, such as "divide by 2," "multiply by 1/2," and "divide by 1/2," and they must see that different models of division are sometimes required to give meaning to such ideas. For example, "divide by 2" can be modeled by a partitioning model ("separate the amount into two equal quantities"), but "divide by 1/2" is more appropriately represented by a repeated-subtraction model:

"You made $2\frac{3}{4}$ gallons of lemonade. How many $\frac{1}{2}$ -gallon bottles can you fill?"

$$\left(2\frac{3}{4} \div \frac{1}{2} = 5, \text{ with a remainder of } \frac{1}{4} \text{ gallon} \right)$$

Encouraging students to estimate and evaluate the reasonableness of the results of their computations is important in helping them expand their number sense.

As students' algebraic concepts grow during grades 6–8, they will also frequently face computations involving variables, and they will need to extend their understanding of the operations and their properties to encompass simplification of and operations with algebraic expressions. Understanding the inverse relationship between addition and subtraction, between multiplication and division, and between "square" and "square root" will be important in such tasks.

In grades 9–12, students should go beyond producing the results of specific computations to generalize about operations and their properties and to relate them to functions and their graphs. For example, they should describe and compare the behavior of functions such as $f(x) = 2x$, $g(x) = x + 2$, $h(x) = x^2$, or $j(x) = \sqrt{x}$. They should reason about number relations, describing, for instance, the value of $a \cdot b$ where a and b are positive numbers and $a + b = 50$. They should understand and correctly apply the results of operating with positive or negative numbers when they are working with both equations and inequalities.

In addition, high school students should learn to perform operations in other systems. They should find vector sums in the plane, add and multiply matrices, or use multiplicative reasoning to represent counting problems and combinatorics.

Computing fluently and making reasonable estimates

Although an understanding of numbers and the meanings of the various operations is essential, it is insufficient unless it is accompanied by the development of computational proficiency and a sense of the reasonableness of computational results. Computational skills emerge in the prekindergarten and early elementary years in conjunction with students' developing understanding of whole numbers and counting.

Young children's earliest computational strategies usually involve counting. As they think about number problems involving addition or subtraction, young students devise different solution schemes, and teachers should listen carefully to their students' explanations of these thinking strategies. Encouraging children to explain their methods and discussing different students' strategies with the class helps students deepen their understanding of numbers and operations and refine their computational abilities.

At first, young children rely heavily on physical objects to represent numerical situations and relationships, and they use such objects to model their addition and subtraction results. Over time, they learn to represent the same problems symbolically, and eventually they carry out the computations mentally or with paper and pencil, without needing the actual physical objects. Students should have enough experience and practice to master the basic one-digit addition and subtraction combinations, and they should combine that knowledge with their understanding of base-ten numeration so that, by the end of grade 2, they can add and subtract with two-digit numbers.

As students become more proficient with addition and subtraction, teachers can help them examine the efficiency and generalizability of their invented strategies and can lead them to an understanding of standard computational algorithms. When students understand the procedures that they are employing, they are able to carry them out with accuracy and efficiency.

In grades 3–5, students should extend their knowledge of basic number combinations to include single-digit multiplication and division facts, and by the end of the upper elementary years they should be able to compute fluently with whole numbers. As students develop their computational proficiency, teachers should guide them in examining and explaining their various approaches and in understanding algorithms for addition, subtraction, multiplication, and division and employing them effectively. In turn, teachers must understand that there is more than one algorithm for each of the operations, and they should recognize that the algorithms that are meaningful to students may not be the ones that have traditionally been taught or that some people have come to assume offer "the right way" to solve a problem.

In grades 3–5, students are beginning to work with larger numbers, and it is important for them to develop a strong sense of the reasonableness of a computational result and a facility in estimating results before computing. It will often be appropriate for students to use calculators when they are working with larger numbers. At other times, paper and pencil may be appropriate, or it may be reasonable for teachers to expect mental computation. Teachers and students should discuss various situations to assist students in developing good judgment about when to use mental arithmetic, paper and pencil, or technology for whole-number computation.

Other aspects of computational fluency in the 3–5 grade band involve understanding the associative, commutative, and distributive properties and seeing how those properties can be used to simplify a computation. Students at this level will also encounter problems that require the introduction of order-of-operations conventions.

While students in grades 3–5 are honing their skills with whole-number computation, they also will be spending a great deal of time developing an understanding of fractions and decimals. However, computing with rational numbers should not be the focus of their attention yet. Rather, students should apply their understanding of fractions and decimals and the properties of the operations to problems that include fractions or decimals. For example, "How many sheets of construction paper will Jackie need to make 16 Halloween decorations if each decoration uses $2\frac{1}{4}$ sheets of paper?" General procedures for calculating with rational numbers and integers will be the focus of instruction in the next grade band.

In grades 6–8, students learn methods for computing with fractions and decimals as extensions of their understanding of rational numbers and their facility in computing with whole numbers. As with whole-number computation, students develop an understanding of computing with fractions, decimals, and integers by considering problems in context, making estimates of reasonable expectations for the results, devising and explaining methods that make sense to them, and comparing their strategies with those of others as well as with standard algorithms. When calculating with fractions and decimals, students must learn to assess situations and decide whether an exact answer is required or whether an estimate is appropriate. They should also develop useful benchmarks to help them assess the reasonableness of results when they are calculating with rational numbers, integers, and percents. Computational fluency at the middle grades also includes a facility in reasoning about and solving problems involving proportions and rates.

In grades 9–12, students should extend their computational proficiency to real numbers and should confidently choose among mental mathematics, paper-and-pencil calculations, and computations with technology to obtain results that offer an appropriate degree of precision. They should perform complex calculations involving powers and roots, vectors, and matrices, as well as real numbers, and they should exhibit a well-developed number sense in judging the reasonableness of calculations, including calculations performed with the aid of technology.

Numbers and Operations in the Mathematics Curriculum

Without numbers and operations there would be no mathematics. Accordingly, the mathematics curriculum must foster the development of both number sense and computational fluency across the entire pre-K–12 continuum. The Number and Operations Standard describes the core of understanding and proficiency that students are expected to attain, and a curriculum that leads to the outcomes envisioned in this Standard must be coherent, developmental, focused, and well articulated across the grades. At all levels, students should develop a true understanding of numbers and operations that will undergird their development of computational fluency.

The *Navigating through Number and Operations* books provide insight into the ways in which the fundamental ideas of number and operations can develop over the pre-K–12 years. These Navigations volumes, however, do not—and cannot—undertake to describe a complete curriculum for number and operations. The concepts described in the Number and Operations Standard regularly apply in other mathematical contexts related to the Algebra, Geometry, Measurement, and Data Analysis and Probability Standards. Activities such as those described in the four *Navigating through Number and Operations* books reinforce and enhance understanding of the other mathematics strands, just as those other strands lend context and meaning to number sense and computation.

The development of mathematical literacy relies on deep understanding of numbers and operations as set forth in *Principles and Standards for School Mathematics*. These *Navigations* volumes are presented as a guide to help educators set a course for the successful implementation of this essential Standard.

NAVIGATING *through* NUMBER *and* OPERATIONS

Chapter 1
Fractions, Decimals, and Percents

Important Mathematical Ideas

Principles and Standards for School Mathematics (NCTM 2000) recommends that students in grades 6–8 deepen their understanding of and facility with fractions, decimals, and percents. They should also develop their ability to solve problems that involve rational numbers. Thus, students should understand that 2/5, 40/100, 0.40 and 40% represent the same number, be able to translate from one representational form to another, and recognize that one representational form may be more appropriate than another in a particular context.

However, research shows that many students struggle with these concepts. Kilpatrick, Swafford, and Findell (2001, p. 101) identify moving between fractions and decimals as "perhaps the deepest translation problem in pre-K to grade 8 mathematics" and go on to say that "successful translation requires an understanding of rational numbers as well as decimal and fractional notation—each of which is a significant and multifaceted idea in its own right." The results of the 1996 National Assessment of Educational Progress echo those findings. On the assessment, fewer than 60 percent of students in grade 12 responded correctly to tasks that assessed knowledge of the relationship between decimals and fractions (Wearne and Kouba 2000).

One cause of students' confusion about rational numbers is the "rush to symbol manipulation," which occurs when students learn algorithms

"Teachers can help students deepen their understanding of rational numbers by presenting problems ... that call for flexible thinking.... At the heart of flexibility in working with rational numbers is a solid understanding of different representations for fractions, decimals, and percents."

(NCTM 2000, p. 215)

Wearne and Kouba (2000; available on the CD-ROM) analyze students' understanding of and facility with rational numbers.

A task such as the next activity, Fund-Raiser, offers a way to assess students' current knowledge of rational numbers.

before also developing an underlying understanding of the concepts (Lappan et al. 1998). When that happens, students know the rules but do not understand why a rule "works" or how to make sense of situations in which they can apply no specific rule. As a result of learning algorithms this way, students often struggle to explain their reasoning or solve problems that involve more than one step (Wearne and Kouba 2000).

The ability to "move around flexibly in the world of rational numbers" contributes to students' understanding of proportionality and opens the door to high school mathematics and science (Lamon 1999, p. 3). Several important ideas related to developing this flexibility with rational numbers should guide your selection of mathematical activities for middle-grades students:

- Fractions, decimals, and percents are different ways of representing rational numbers.
- Connections between fraction and decimal symbolism can facilitate an understanding of both.
- Visual models can enhance students' understanding of rational numbers by providing concrete representations of abstract ideas.
- Solving applied problems requires skill in using fractions, decimals, and percents flexibly and meaningfully.
- Mathematical thinking should be communicated to peers and teachers coherently and clearly.

Although mathematical content is one important criterion for selecting mathematical activities for students, it is the nature of the tasks to which students are exposed that will determine what students learn (NCTM 1991). As Stein and Smith (1998) point out, "Tasks that ask students to perform a memorized procedure in a routine manner lead to one type of opportunity for student thinking; tasks that require students to think conceptually and that stimulate students to make connections lead to a different set of opportunities for student thinking" (p. 269).

Hence, if the goal is to develop students' capacity to think, reason, and solve problems, then it is critical to engage students in solving cognitively complex tasks (Stein and Lane 1996). Making the effort to present such tasks is particularly important in the domain of rational numbers. All too often, routine activities and standardized tests require students only to apply previously learned rules and procedures—not to think or reason.

What Might Students Already Know about These Ideas?

Students enter middle school with both formal and informal knowledge about rational numbers from their school and life experiences. By the end of fifth grade, students should have an understanding of part-to-whole relationships and be able to recognize and generate forms of commonly used fractions, decimals, and percents (NCTM 2000).

Fund-Raiser

Goal

- Assess students'—
  - ability to use fractions, decimals, or percents to represent a shaded region in terms of the unit whole;
  - ability to use a visual representation of a part-to-whole relationship to determine the fractional part represented;
  - ability to solve a contextual problem involving rational numbers;
  - ability to communicate mathematical thinking in oral and written form.

Materials

For each student—

- A copy of the blackline master "The Fund-Raising Thermometer"
- A calculator (optional)

For the teacher—

- A transparency of the blackline master "The Fund-Raising Thermometer" or copies on large sheets of paper

p. 114

Fig. **1.1.**

The fund-raising thermometer

Activity

Begin the activity by asking your students what they know about fund-raisers. Be sure that the students understand the idea of setting a fund-raising goal and tracking progress toward that goal. Distribute a copy of the activity sheet, "The Fund-Raising Thermometer," to each student. Discuss with the class how a thermometer might be used to record progress toward a goal. Review the activity with the students and ask them to work individually on the activity sheet. For question 1, the students should use the thermometer (see fig. 1.1) to describe *everything* they can about the fund-raiser from the figure and the context of the problem. For question 2, the students should turn over their activity sheets to write an announcement of fund-raising progress for a sixth-grade officer to read over the school's public address system. Observe the students as they work to see how they approach the problem.

Discussion

Have student volunteers come forward to explain what they have determined about the fund-raiser. If possible, have them explain their strategies and thinking by using a transparency of the fund-raising thermometer or copies drawn to scale on large sheets of paper.

This class discussion will give you additional information to assess what your students already know about rational numbers. As the students explain what they have determined about the fund-raiser from their explorations of the thermometer, take notes on how they are approaching and solving the problem. Some questions to consider include the following:

This activity has been adapted from Lappan et al. (1998).

- How do the students measure the shaded portion of the thermometer?
- What informal strategies do the students use to determine the fractional part represented by the shaded portion of the thermometer?
- Do the students talk about the shaded area of the thermometer as being one of four equal parts?
- How do the students use the fact that the shaded area is 1/4 of the goal to determine how much money remains to be raised?
- Do the students relate the portion of the goal raised to the fact that the sixth-grade class raised 1/4 of the goal in 1/5 of the allotted time?
- What representations of rational numbers do the students use spontaneously in describing the poster sale?
- What strategies do the students use to describe the part of the sales goal of $300 that has been reached and the part that remains to be raised?
- What aspects of the problem appear to be difficult for the students?

You are likely to see a wide variety of approaches. However, the answers to the questions above and the students' written work on the activity sheet will give you valuable insights into the students' knowledge of and flexibility with rational numbers in an applied context.

Examples from one class that undertook this activity are quite telling. Nearly all the students in this particular sixth-grade class realized that the thermometer needed to be divided into equal parts and that they needed to represent the shaded area of the thermometer as a part of the whole thermometer. All students, however, did not use the same strategy. Many students began by measuring the length of the shaded portion of the thermometer by using their fingers, pencils, or rulers. They then repeated the measure until they reached the goal of $300. One student, Tamika, used such an approach, referring to the repeated measures of the shaded portion as sections. "I estimated how long each section was by using my pinky finger. I measured the first section, and then I made all the other sections," she explained. Some students, however, started with the whole thermometer and broke it into "chunks" of $5, $20, or $100 (often without using precise measures) instead of beginning with the shaded area and using this quantity to divide the thermometer into equal segments.

Nearly all the students were able to represent the shaded area of the thermometer as a fraction of the goal and determine an appropriate dollar value for day 2 of the poster sale. Even students using incorrect fractions understood how to use them correctly to calculate the dollar amount earned. Students who correctly identified the shaded area as 1/4 of the goal typically found it by calculating 300 ÷ 4 (by hand or with the aid of the calculator) or by mentally calculating that "half of $300 is $150; half of $150 is $75." In addition, some of these students also identified the shaded area as representing 25 percent of the goal. A few students, like Maria (see fig. 1.2), represented each of the four equal sections of the thermometer in terms of a fraction, decimal, percent,

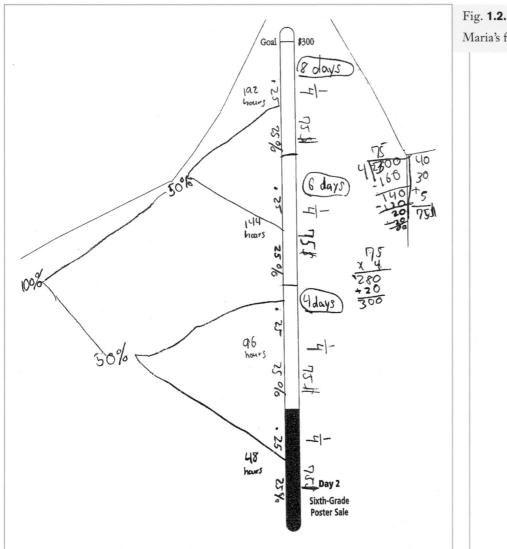

Fig. **1.2.**

Maria's fund-raising thermometer

dollar amount, and number of days. Her unwarranted assumption that the cash flow would be uniform probably arose from her initial division of the thermometer into quarters.

Some students successfully determined the amount represented by the shaded area but did not explain how they did so. For example, Beth divided the thermometer into three equal pieces and labeled the first two sections $100 and $200, respectively. She proceeded to identify the shaded area correctly as 1/4 and the dollar value for day 2 of the poster sale as $75. It is not clear, however, why she divided the thermometer into thirds or how she determined the value of the shaded area.

The quality of the students' announcements varied also. Some students in this class did not write the announcements. This omission raised questions about their ability to use the data that they generated to answer the question and their ability to communicate in writing. Of the students who wrote announcements, some omitted important information. For example, Keisha indicated that the sixth-grade class had earned $75, or 25 percent of its goal, but she did not indicate what part of the goal remained to be raised. Although Keisha stated, "I believe that the end of the sale will be on the eighth day and they will reach their goal," she did not state that the goal could be achieved in

Fig. **1.3.**

Announcements by William (top) and Tanya (bottom)

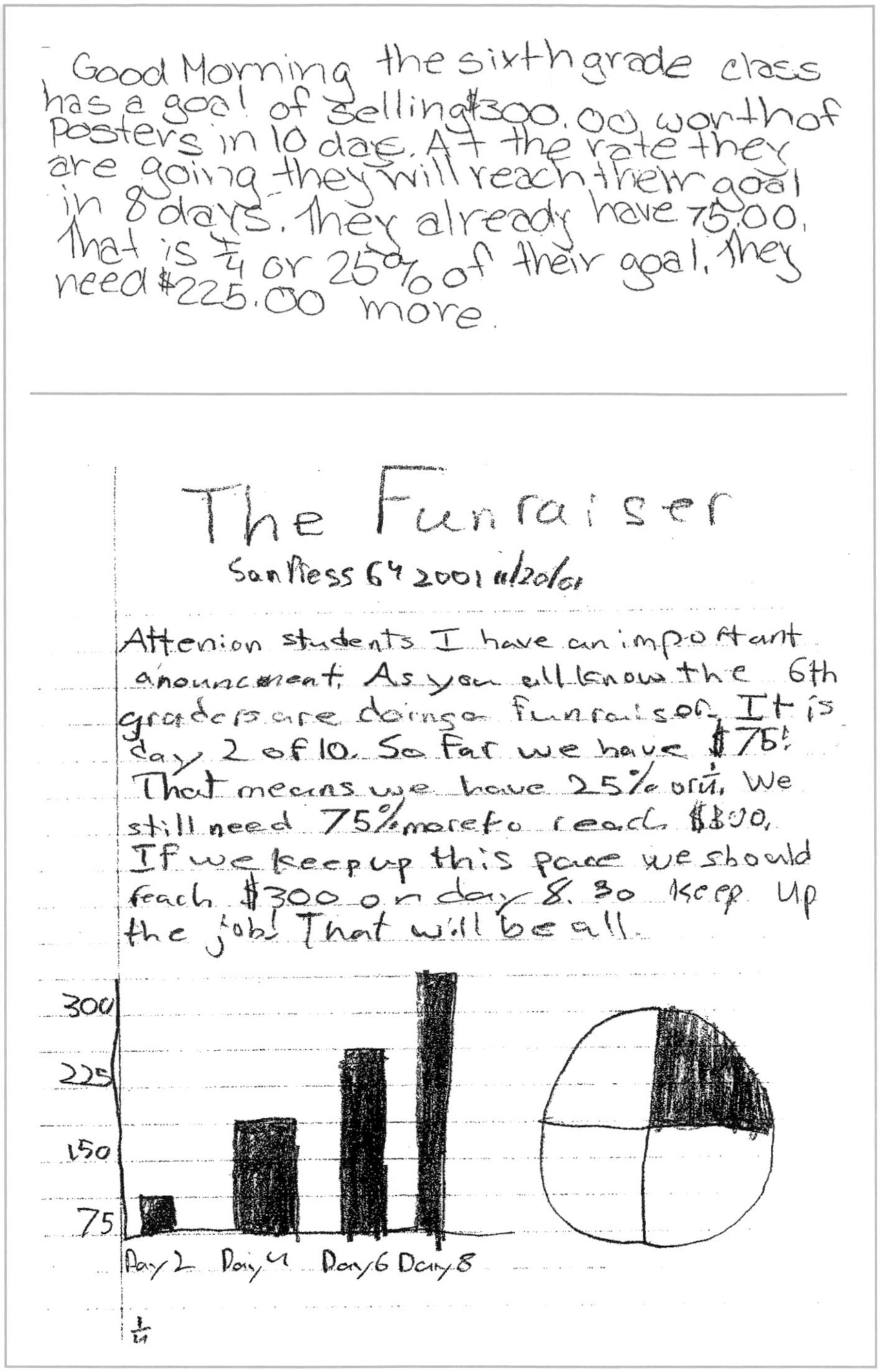

Good Morning the sixth grade class has a goal of selling $300.00 worth of Posters in 10 das. At the rate they are going they will reach their goal in 8 days. They already have 75.00. That is ¼ or 25% of their goal, they need $225.00 more.

The Funraiser

San Pess 6ª 2001 11/20/01

Attension students I have an impoAtant anouncement. As you ell know the 6th graders are doing a funraisor. It is day 2 of 10. So far we have $75! That means we have 25% orй. We still need 75% more to read $300. If we keep up this pace we should reach $300 on day 8. So keep up the job! That will be all.

eight days *if* they continued to sell posters *at the same rate* as the first two days of the sale. A few students, like William and Tanya, wrote announcements that went beyond what was requested. They both said that the goal would be reached by day eight if the students continued to sell posters at the same rate or pace (see fig. 1.3).

Activities like Fund-Raiser are designed to assess students' thinking as well as offer insight into students' current conceptions. To ensure that the chosen task generates valuable information, however, keep in mind these guidelines:

- The mathematical task should involve students in thinking and reasoning.

- You should let the students work through the problem on their own rather than tell them how to do it when they experience difficulty.
- You should review the students' work not to evaluate their performance but to make decisions regarding subsequent instruction.

After the teacher reviewed the work of the students in the class described above, she planned to give the students additional opportunities to communicate about mathematics and to solve applied problems. Furthermore, from her students' work, she could see that although some students used different forms of rational numbers for a common fraction (for example, 1/4 = 0.25 = 25%), it was not clear what her students understood about the relationships among these forms. She planned further work on part-to-whole relationships with an emphasis on developing the students' flexibility with fractions, decimals, and percents. Similarly, once you complete this task with your students, you should be able to make sound decisions about where to take your instruction next.

Selected Instructional Activities

The activities in this chapter are intended to help students develop an understanding of and flexibility with fractions, decimals, and percents. The first two activities—Science Fair and A Handy Survey—give students opportunities to work with fractions, decimals, and percents in different applied contexts. Through these activities, students must decide how they will represent rational numbers. The problems involve several steps and require flexible thinking. Thus, students must develop a deeper understanding of the meaning of the rules and procedures.

The next two activities—Representing Shaded Areas of Rectangular Grids and Shading Areas of Rectangular Grids—emphasize the links among fractions, decimals, and percents and help students see that each form can represent a different way of expressing the same quantity. The students practice expressing quantities in interchangeable forms and selecting and using the representation that is the most appropriate for solving a given problem. They use rectangular grids to verify visually the equivalence of fraction, decimal, and percent representations of the same shaded portion of a given whole. In Representing Shaded Areas of Rectangular Grids, the students see the shaded portion of a grid's area and express it as a decimal, fraction, or percentage. In Shading Areas of Rectangular Grids, the situation is reversed—the students must shade a rectangular area to correspond with a given decimal, fraction, or percentage. Notice how switching the information that you give students with what they must find increases students' flexibility and the range of alternative approaches that the students use to relate fractions, decimals, and percents. This approach increases both the complexity of the problem and the extent to which it helps students enrich their concepts of the representational forms for rational numbers.

At the end of the chapter, the section Extensions discusses different resources and ideas for extending students' learning of the concepts.

Science Fair

Goals

- Use different forms of rational numbers interchangeably
- Recognize the need to find a common basis for comparing quantities of different sizes
- Communicate mathematical thinking

Materials

For each student—

- A copy of the blackline master "Science Fair"
- A calculator

For the teacher—

- A transparency of the auditorium rectangle (drawn to scale) from the blackline master "Science Fair"
- An overhead calculator (optional)

pp. 115–16

Activity

Distribute a copy of the activity sheet "Science Fair" to each student. Three middle schools are planning to hold a joint science fair, and they will allocate space in the auditorium according to the number of students in each school. Have the students work in pairs to complete questions 1 and 2, which ask them to divide a rectanglar auditorium to show the space that each school will have and to tell what fraction of the rectangle that space represents. Then lead a class discussion of the students' solutions and reasoning. This discussion will give you an opportunity to discuss any difficulties or misconceptions and give students a chance to reconsider their fractions before completing questions 3 and 4.

Discussion

To divide the rectangle correctly, the students must recognize that the space allocated to a school is proportional to its enrollment. Although your students might have an intuitive sense that Bret Harte Middle School gets the most space and Kennedy Middle School gets the least, they must find a way to quantify the space.

The students will probably find several different ways to divide the rectangle correctly. Examples from an actual classroom illustrate some of the approaches and thinking that you might see. For example, figure 1.4 shows that Jamal allocated half the space to Bret Harte Middle School, reasoning that half the students attend the school. He then divided the remaining half of the rectangle into ten sections and gave six to Malcolm X Middle School and four to Kennedy Middle School. Although an approach like Jamal's leads to a successful division of the auditorium, it could cause difficulties for some students, who might then write the fractions as 1/2 (Bret Harte), 6/10 (Malcolm X), and 4/10 (Kennedy). These students would have failed to realize that Malcolm X's share was 6/10 of 1/2 of the auditorium space (or 6/20),

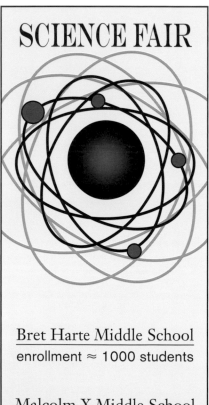

SCIENCE FAIR

Bret Harte Middle School
enrollment ≈ 1000 students

Malcolm X Middle School
enrollment ≈ 600 students

Kennedy Middle School
enrollment ≈ 400 students

that Kennedy's share was 4/10 of 1/2 of the space (or 4/20), and that the total of their fractions (1/2 + 6/10 + 4/10) exceeds 1, or 100 percent. By contrast, Kara's approach, depicted in figure 1.5, shows clearly that the six sections for Malcolm X and the four for Kennedy represent twentieths, not tenths.

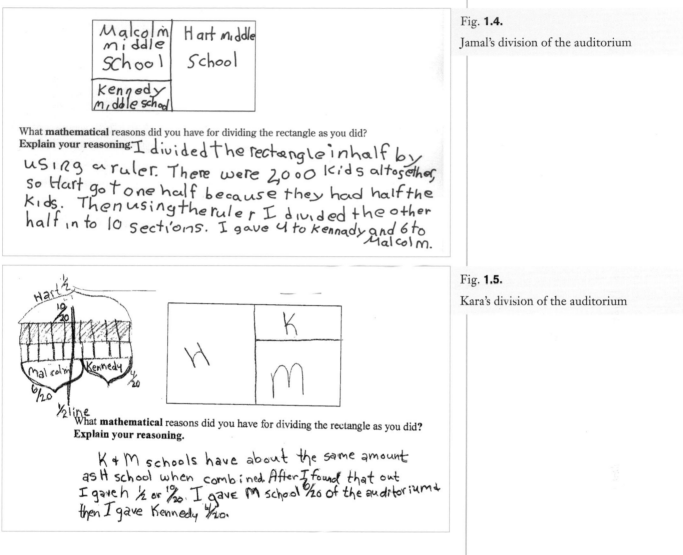

What **mathematical** reasons did you have for dividing the rectangle as you did?
Explain your reasoning. I divided the rectangle in half by using a ruler. There were 2,000 kids altogether, so Hart got one half because they had half the kids. Then using the ruler I divided the other half into 10 sections. I gave 4 to kennedy and 6 to Malcolm.

Fig. **1.4.**

Jamal's division of the auditorium

What **mathematical** reasons did you have for dividing the rectangle as you did?
Explain your reasoning.

K & M schools have about the same amount as H school when combined. After I found that out I gave h ½ or 10/20. I gave M school 6/20 of the auditorium & then I gave Kennedy 4/20.

Fig. **1.5.**

Kara's division of the auditorium

The approach taken by Andrea, shown in figure 1.6, involves identifying 200 as the greatest common factor of 400, 600, and 1000, and determining that there would be ten 200s in 2000. She then drew a 2 × 5

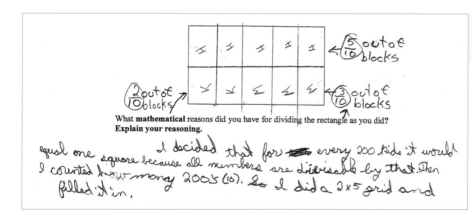

What **mathematical** reasons did you have for dividing the rectangle as you did?
Explain your reasoning.

equal one square because all numbers are divisable by that. Then I counted how many 200's (10). So I did a 2x5 grid and I decided that for every 200 kids it would filled it in.

Fig. **1.6.**

Andrea's division of the auditorium

unit grid, with each cell representing 200 students. She allocated five of the ten blocks to Bret Harte, four to Malcolm X, and two to Kennedy.

Some of the students in this particular class did not realize that the amount of space allocated to a school needed to be proportional to the number of students and that the schools with more students would get more space. These students simply divided the rectangle into three equal parts—giving each school 1/3 of the auditorium. Other students recognized that Bret Harte would receive half the space since that school had half the students, but they then also divided the remaining space equally between Malcolm X and Kennedy.

Discussions of the students' solution strategies often led to other important topics. For example, Roza reasoned that 2000 ÷ 1000 = 2, so Bret Harte should receive 1/2 of the space, and that 2000 ÷ 400 = 5, so Kennedy should receive 1/5 of the space. Not surprisingly, when Roza found that 2000 ÷ 600 = 3.333..., it was more difficult for her to determine an appropriate fractional name for this repeating decimal. Instead of writing the fraction as 1/(3.333...) (following the pattern of the other divisions), she rounded it to 1/3. Her approach led to an interesting class discussion about the difference between 0.30 (the correct allocation for Malcolm X) and 0.333... (Roza's rounded value), with the students recognizing the inequality of the two numbers.

Another student, Robert, divided the rectangle into four equal rows, each of which contained 500 students (see fig. 1.7). Next, he divided one row into five equal pieces, each of which contained 100 students.

Fig. **1.7.**

Robert's division of the auditorium

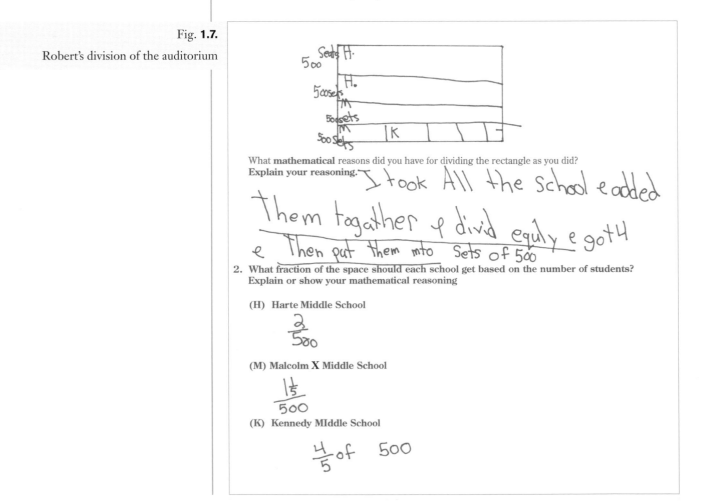

Navigating through Number and Operations in Grades 6–8

Then he assigned two sets of 500 to Bret Harte and one set of 500 to Malcolm X. He went on to distribute one of the sets of 100 to Malcolm X and the remaining four sets of 100 to Kennedy. Although Robert correctly divided the rectangle, he ran into problems when he tried to write the fractional equivalents, and his expressions for Bret Harte and Malcolm X (shown in question 2 of fig. 1.7) were incorrect. This led to another interesting discussion, in which other students in the class helped Robert realize that his expressions represented the number of groups of 500 rather than the fraction of space allotted. (For example, "2/500" represented two groups of 500, or 1000 students.)

Once the students in your class have discussed various approaches to dividing the rectangle and writing fractions, allow them to revise their work before moving on to the remaining questions, which address sharing the cost of the science fair among the three schools. When the students have completed the activity sheet, have a few students share accurate solutions with the class. This presentation can allow the entire class to see models of high-level performance.

The activity Science Fair offers a context for students to consider the meaning of fractional representations for rational numbers and of the equivalence of fractions. Through discussions of the questions, the activity also offers opportunities for discussing other related ideas, such as whether 0.30 and 0.333... are equivalent. The following activity, A Handy Survey, offers another applied context in which students can naturally explore the equivalence of fractions, decimals, and percents.

A Handy Survey

Goals

- Use different forms of rational numbers interchangeably in an applied context
- Communicate mathematical thinking

Materials

For each student—

- A copy of the blackline master "A Handy Survey"
- A calculator

For the teacher—

- An overhead calculator (optional)

Activity

Distribute a copy of the blackline master "A Handy Survey" to each student. A book claims that 10 percent of the population is left-handed. This statistic surprised a group of students, who surveyed twenty students in each of four homerooms (see the margin). Did their survey yield a higher or a lower percentage of left-handed people? Review the activity sheet with your students, and then ask them to work individually to complete it. Discuss their answers and mathematical reasoning in class. This activity gives students a different context—a survey—in which to apply their knowledge of fractions and percents.

Discussion

In this activity, the students must interpret sample data about the number of right- and left-handed students in four different homerooms. Figure 1.8 shows Kaila's approach to comparing the data and

p. 117

Ms. Grey's Homeroom	
Right	19
Left	1
Total	20

Ms. LaRue's Homeroom	
Right	17
Left	3
Total	20

Ms. Davison's Homeroom	
Right	18
Left	2
Total	20

Mr. Fisher's Homeroom	
Right	17
Left	3
Total	20

Fig. **1.8.**

Kaila's work on the activity sheet "A Handy Survey"

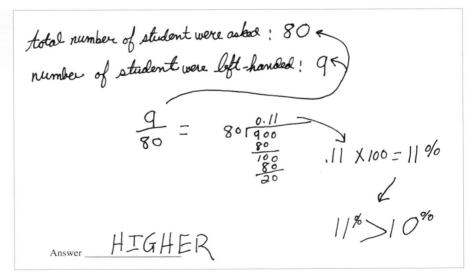

This activity has been adapted from Parke et al. (2004).

determining whether the class survey produced a higher percentage of left-handed people than the given statistic. She began by representing the total number of left-handed students as a fraction (9/80) and converting the fraction to a decimal and a percent. She then compared her calculated percentage (11 percent) to the given percentage (10 percent) and concluded that the survey produced a higher percentage of left-handed students.

Alternatively, a student might begin with the given percentage (10 percent) and determine whether more or fewer than 10 percent of the students in the survey were left-handed. As shown in figure 1.9, Jalin noted that 8 out of 80 would be 10 percent. In the survey, the students found that a total of 9 out of the 80 students surveyed were left-handed. So, Jalin reasoned, the percentage of left-handed students must be greater than the percentage reported in the book. In this instance, Jalin did not calculate a percentage but instead used his knowledge of percents and part-to-whole relationships to solve the problem.

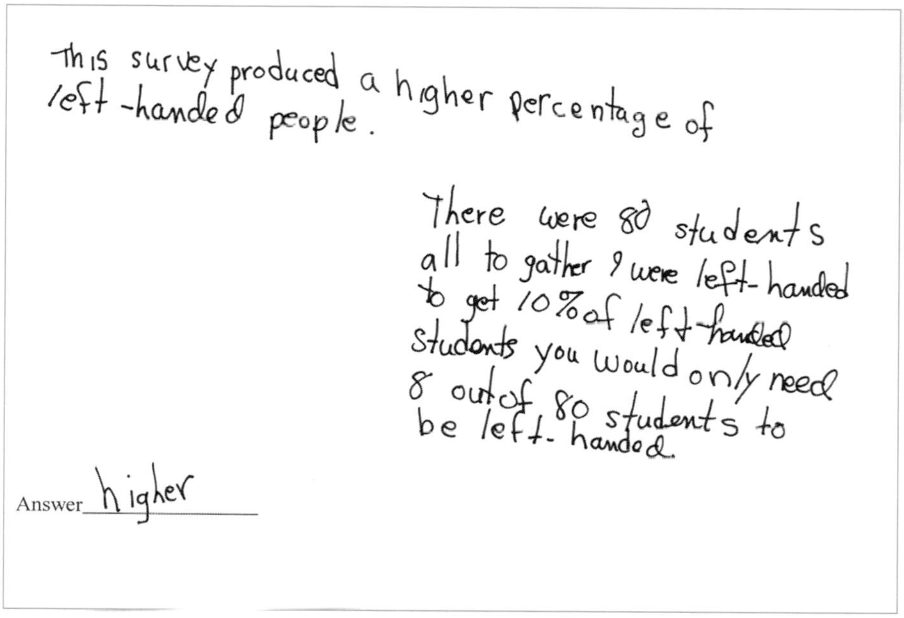
This survey produced a higher percentage of left-handed people.

There were 80 students all to gather 9 were left-handed to get 10% of left-handed students you would only need 8 out of 80 students to be left-handed.

Answer higher

Fig. **1.9.**

Jalin's work on the activity sheet "A Handy Survey"

The next two activities—Representing Shaded Areas of Rectangular Grids and Shading Areas of Rectangular Grids—are adapted from Foreman and Bennett (1996). The activities use rectangular grids to encourage students to make conceptual rather than procedural connections among fractions, decimals, and percents. By showing fraction, decimal, and percent representations for the same shaded portion of a given whole, the students visually verify equivalence.

Representing Shaded Areas of Rectangular Grids

Goals

- Identify shaded regions of rectangular grids by using fractions, decimals, and percents
- Recognize that fractions, decimals, and percents are different ways of representing the same quantity
- Use rectangular grids as tools for making sense of abstract mathematical ideas
- Communicate mathematical thinking

Materials

For each student—

- A copy of the blackline master "Representing Shaded Areas of Rectangular Grids"
- A calculator

For the teacher—

- An overhead projector
- A transparency of the blackline master "Representing Shaded Areas of Rectangular Grids" (or individual transparencies of each rectangular grid from the blackline master)
- An overhead calculator (optional)
- A large sheet of paper (optional)

pp. 118–19

Activity

Group the students in pairs and distribute a copy of the blackline master "Representing Shaded Areas of Rectangular Grids" to each pair. Point out that the students need to express the shaded area of each grid as a fraction, a decimal, and a percentage of the total area. Focus on one grid and walk them through the process if necessary. Stress to the students that they should explain their thinking, and observe the different approaches that the students use to solve the problems.

Discussion

To encourage the students to explore different ways of solving the problems, invite them to present alternative solutions that you have observed. You might want to have an overhead transparency of each figure available to facilitate the students' explanations. It might also be helpful for you to keep a list on the board or a large sheet of paper of the different strategies that the students present. Publicizing these strategies makes them available to all students and allows the students to make easy comparisons of the strategies and their effectiveness in solving different types of problems.

This activity has been adapted from Foreman and Bennett (1996).

1.

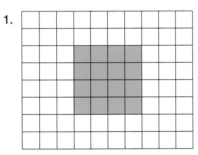

2.

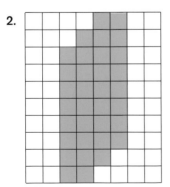

Navigating through Number and Operations in Grades 6–8

Typically, students begin this activity by counting the number of shaded squares and expressing that number as a fraction of the total number of squares in the rectangle. Many students determine the decimal and percent equivalents by dividing the numerator by the denominator (to get the decimal) and then moving the decimal point two places to the right (to get the percent). But this approach is not the only way. In your class discussion, encourage the students to present alternative approaches or demonstrate one or two of them yourself.

The following examples show how students in one sixth-grade class worked through this activity. One student, Natalie, gave the solution to grid 2 as 34/80 (the number of shaded squares over the total number of squares). She explained that 34/80 was equal to 0.425 and 42.5 percent. When asked to explain where her answer came from, she said that she had "divided the bottom into the top" by using a calculator, got a decimal, and then moved the decimal point over two places to obtain the percent. When another student in the class questioned how she had gotten 42.5, Natalie used an overhead calculator to demonstrate the procedure for dividing 34 by 80.

The teacher asked whether anyone solved the problem another way. Deanna suggested that 34/80 was the same as 340/800, and that dividing the numerator and the denominator by 8 would give 42.5/100. When the teacher asked why she had done it that way, Deanna replied that she made the bottom a multiple of 100 because it was easier to think about.

At this point, the teacher decided to introduce an alternative explanation for grid 2. He asked the students, "If you have 80 squares, would each square be worth more than, less than, or the same as 1 percent?" After some discussion, the students agreed that each square would be worth more than one percent, since there were only 80 squares over which to distribute 100 percent. The teacher then asked how much each square would "get." One student suggested using a calculator to find out. The teacher noted that if they distributed 1 percent to each of the 80 squares, they would have 20 percent left over to divide evenly among the 80 squares. A student then suggested that each square would get an additional $\frac{1}{4}$ percent. Next, the teacher asked how they could find the percent of the region that was shaded if they knew that each square was worth $1\frac{1}{4}$ percent. Another student suggested that they multiply $34 \times 1\frac{1}{4}$. Rather than multiply $34 \times 1\frac{1}{4}$ in their heads by multiplying $(34 \times 1) + (34 \times \frac{1}{4})$ and reasoning that the product would be $34 + 8\frac{1}{2}$, the students used their calculators. They determined that this approach would give them the same answer as the previous methods.

The teacher summarized their methods so far: "We've got Natalie's method of using a calculator. We've got Deanna's method of finding a number that can be made into a multiple of 100 so we can reduce it to some number out of 100. And we have the method of finding what percent each square is worth and then multiplying by the number of squares."

When the class moved on to subsequent problems, additional strategies surfaced. For grid 3, Michael began by subtracting the 16 unshaded squares from the total of 64 to determine that 48 were shaded. He wrote 48/64 = 6/8 = 3/4. He explained that he multiplied

The description of the work of this sixth-grade class comes from "The Case of Randy Harris," which appears in *Improving Instruction in Rational Numbers and Proportionality: Using Cases to Transform Mathematics Teaching and Learning,* vol. 1 (Smith et al. 2005).

3.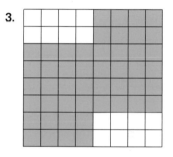

4.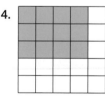

5.

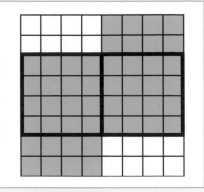

Fig. 1.10.

Peter's subdivision of the shaded area for grid 3

3/4 by 100 to get 75 percent, and then moved the decimal to get 0.75. The teacher commented that Michael had done the problem by reducing a fraction to something more understandable. In yet another approach (see fig. 1.10), Peter pointed out that by dividing the shared area "just right," he could "see" the 75 percent on the diagram. Using the diagram, Peter explained that combining the shaded part in the top right (a 2 × 4 unit region) with the shaded part in the bottom left (another 2 × 4 region) gives a 4 × 4 region. The other shaded part, he explained, could be subdivided into two 4 × 4 regions. The unshaded part would also be a 4 × 4 region if the two sections were combined. Therefore, Peter argued, the diagram showed four 4 × 4 sections and three of them, or 75 percent, were shaded.

Still another way to emphasize the connections among fractions, decimals, and percents is to have the students think about a rectangular grid as though it were divided into 100 equal parts. For example, the students are likely to represent the shaded area in grid 4 (shown in fig. 1.11) as the fraction 12/25. By subdividing each square in the grid into four smaller squares, the fraction can be represented as 48/100 or 48 percent.

Fig. 1.11.

Grid 4 (left) subdivided (right) to show the equivalence of 12/25 (left) and 48/100 (right)

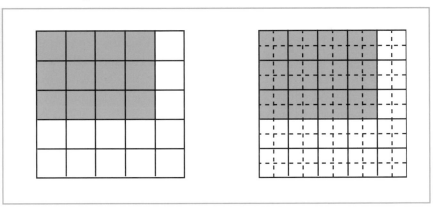

Previous experiences that your students have had with activities like this are likely to affect their readiness to make connections among fractions, decimals, and percents. The sixth-grade class described in this activity had just begun a unit on percents and had used rectangular grids of different dimensions (starting with a 10 × 10 grid) to develop an understanding of percent and how they could represent different percents (75%, $37\frac{1}{2}$%, 147%, 0.25%). Those same students had practiced relating fractions to decimals in fifth grade by using 10 × 10 grids and had used base-ten pieces to develop an understanding of the meanings of decimal operations.

This activity demonstrates how a challenging task can support students' engagement in thinking about important mathematical ideas. To achieve that end, be sure to focus the discussion on sense making and push the students to make connections between their methods for solving the problems and the underlying concepts that give those methods meaning. Furthermore, rather than discourage the students from using algorithmic approaches, encourage them to find more than one way to solve a problem and to make connections among approaches.

6.

7.

8.

Navigating through Number and Operations in Grades 6–8

Shading Areas of Rectangular Grids

Goals

- Shade regions of rectangular grids to represent given fractions, decimals, and percents
- Recognize that fractions, decimals, and percents can represent the same quantity in different ways
- Develop general strategies—such as "chunking" and unit rate—for representing rational numbers on a rectangular grid
- Use rectangular grids as tools for making sense of abstract mathematical ideas
- Communicate mathematical thinking

Materials

For each student—

- A copy of the blackline master "Shading Areas of Rectangular Grids"
- A calculator

For the teacher—

- An overhead projector (optional)
- A transparency of the "Shading Areas of Rectangular Grids" blackline master (optional)
- An overhead calculator (optional)

p. 120

Activity

Distribute a copy of the "Shading Areas of Rectangular Grids" activity sheet to each student. In this activity, the students shade an area on a grid to represent a given fraction, decimal, or percent. Have the students work in groups of four to complete the activity sheet. Visit each of the groups and provide direction as needed. It might be helpful to demonstrate some of the students' solution strategies on an overhead transparency.

Discussion

The students will probably find these problems challenging. Rather than shading a part of the grid represented by a whole number, they must shade a region represented by a fraction, decimal, or percent. Furthermore, the grids vary in size and are not standard 10 × 10 unit grids. Thus, this activity tests students' flexibility in using what they know about fractions, decimals, and percents to solve problems in unfamiliar situations.

This activity is adapted from Foreman and Bennett (1996).

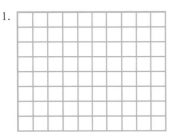

1.

What portion = 0.725 of the region?

What fraction is this?

What percentage?

2.

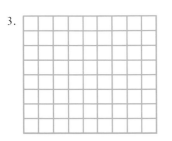

What portion = $\frac{3}{8}$ of the region?

What percentage is this?

What decimal number?

3.

What portion = 87.5% of the region?

What fraction is this?

What decimal number?

The students will probably need some guidance from you as they answer the questions and seek to understand the different possible strategies. Here are some suggestions that might help you support their work and reasoning and help you facilitate class discussions:

- The students might tend to rely primarily on arithmetic procedures for equating fractions, decimals, and percents and might seem unable to use the diagrams to think about the problems. If these difficulties develop, help focus their attention on the rows, columns, or other subsections of the grid to think about what portion they should shade. For example, in problem 1, help the students recognize that each column of the grid represents 1/10, 0.10 or 10 percent of the total grid. Similarly, in problem 2, the students should see that two rows of the grid represent 25 percent of the total grid. Once they begin to see the grids in this way, they should be on their way to figuring out the solutions.

- If some students struggle to find a starting point, ask one or two groups to present and explain their solutions to the first problem. Seeing solution strategies might help the students who are stuck. Furthermore, those demonstrated strategies will then be available for other students to use on subsequent problems, if appropriate.

- Watch for a common error—treating the grids as if they were 10×10 grids. If the students produce incorrect solutions that suggest that they made this error (e.g., shading 72 1/2 squares in problem 1), help them focus on the total number of squares in the grid and the relative number of those squares that they need to shade. For example, in problem 1 the grid contains 80 squares rather than 100. If the students shaded 72.5 of the squares, then the shading would appear in more than 7 out of every set of 8 squares. Such shading would be more than 0.725, or 72.5 percent, which would correspond to having only about 7 out of 10 squares shaded.

After the students have attempted all the problems, have them share solution strategies and approaches in a class discussion. Try to elicit responses that illustrate general solution strategies. For example, for problem 1, one general strategy that the students could use is "chunking." In a chunking approach, students partition the grid into 10 columns, each of which represents 0.10, or 10 percent, of the grid. Then they can determine that the 8 squares in the column are equal to 0.10, so two squares must be equal to 0.025 (or 0.10 ÷ 4). This will lead them to conclude that they need to shade 7 rows and 2 squares to get 0.725.

An alternative general strategy for problem 1 is to work with a unit rate. In this approach, the students determine that if the entire grid of 80 squares is 100 percent, then each square in the grid must represent 80 ÷ 100, or 1.25 percent. Next, they can reason that if each square is 1.25 percent, then four squares represent 5 percent. Thus, each row is 10 percent, and they need to shade 7 rows plus 2 squares.

You should also discuss the relative strengths and weaknesses of various approaches and methods in different situations. For example, a unit-rate approach works well in problem 1 because it is easy to distribute 100 percent over 80 squares and see that an individual square corresponds to 1.25 percent. In problem 2, however, this approach is less useful because it is not so easy to distribute 100 percent over 96 squares; in this instance, an individual square corresponds to 1.041666... percent.

Extensions

In the previous two activities, notice how reversing the direction of a mathematical activity increases both the complexity of the problem and the extent to which students can enrich their concepts of the representational forms for rational numbers. Switching the information that you give students with what you are asking them to find increases students' flexibility and the range of approaches that the students use to relate fractions, decimals, and percents.

The activities in chapter 1 support students' development of a conceptual understanding of the connections among fractions, decimals, and percents. If your students need more experiences, you can use many other activities to help them make these connections. For example, you might try focusing the students' attention on reasoning about the relative sizes of quantities and finding meaningful ways to compare them. You could pose problems such as the following:

- "Is 1/5 greater than 25%?" (No, 1/5 is equal to 20%.)
- "What is the order, from smallest to largest, of this set of numbers: 1/8, 10%, 1/9, and 0.11?" (10%, 0.11, 1/9, 1/8)

The CD-ROM accompanying this book features a wealth of resources to help you extend the concepts developed in this chapter. The readings highlight research, activities, and discussions of best practices for helping students develop an understanding of rational numbers. The readings also explore the individual domains of fractions, decimals, and percents more deeply.

One helpful resource is an analysis of the teaching of fractions by Lamon (2001). She details findings of her longitudinal study of children's development of meanings and operations with rational numbers. She also discusses approaches to teaching fractions that go beyond the predominant part-whole instructional approach. Figure 1.12 shows a set of problems that illustrate these approaches.

Technology can also play an important role in illuminating for students the concepts of rational numbers. The applets on the CD demonstrate the role that technology can play in developing students' facility with and fluency in identifying equivalent representations for rational numbers. The applet Scale 'n Pop (shown in fig. 1.13) helps students investigate the effect of multiplying an integer by a fraction and the effect of the numerator and denominator on the magnitude of a fraction. The applet challenges students to use a scale factor to size balloons. They must find a fraction that will inflate or deflate a balloon to a size small enough to travel through a passageway yet still large enough to be punctured by a pair of nails.

 Susan J. Lamon analyzes the teaching of fractions in "Presenting and Representing: From Fractions to Rational Numbers" (2001; available on the CD-ROM).

Fig. **1.12.**

Fraction problems adapted from Lamon (2001, pp. 146–47)

1. Does the shaded area [of the circle] show 1 ($\frac{3}{8}$ pie), 3 ($\frac{1}{8}$ pies), or $1\frac{1}{2}$ ($\frac{1}{4}$ pies)? Does it matter?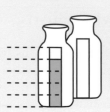

2. You have 16 candies. You divide them into 4 groups, select one group, and make it three times its size. What single operation would have accomplished the same result?

3. You have taken only one drink of juice, represented by the unshaded area in the jar. How much of your day's supply, consisting of two bottles of juice, do you have left?

4. If it takes 9 people $1\frac{1}{2}$ hours to do a job, how long will it take 6 people to do it?

5. Without using common denominators, name three fractions between $\frac{7}{9}$ and $\frac{7}{8}$.

6. Yesterday Alicia jogged 2 laps around the track in 5 minutes, and today she jogged 3 laps around the track in 8 minutes. On her faster day, assuming that she could maintain her pace, how long would it have taken her to do 5 laps?

7. Here are the dimensions of some photos: (a) 9 cm × 10 cm, (b) 10 cm × 12 cm, (c) 6 cm × 8 cm, (d) 5 cm × 6.5 cm, and (e) 8 cm × 9.6 cm. Which one of them might be an enlargement of which other one?

Fig. **1.13.**

A sample screen from the applet Scale 'n Pop (applet created by and used with the permission of Math Forum; figure does not show applet's actual colors)

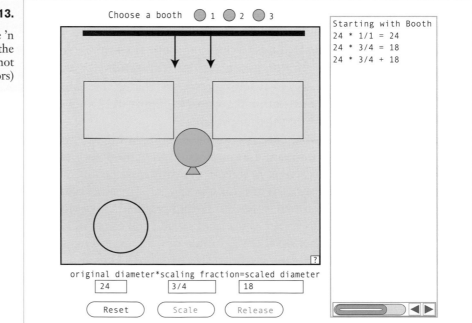

The applet Fraction Four (see fig. 1.14) demonstrates how to build on students' conceptual understanding to promote their facility and fluency in translating rational numbers from one form to another. Two students, playing as Player Red and Player Blue, must give a fraction equivalent for a percent or a decimal equivalent for a fraction. The applet rewards each timely, correct answer with a colored chip that the player can add to the game board. The first player to get four colored chips in a row (horizontally, vertically, or diagonally) wins the game. (Chips are shown here as black and gray instead of red and blue.)

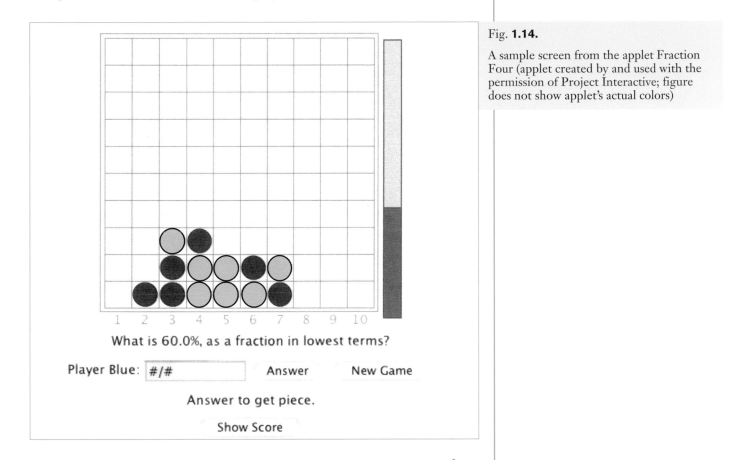

Fig. 1.14.

A sample screen from the applet Fraction Four (applet created by and used with the permission of Project Interactive; figure does not show applet's actual colors)

Conclusion

Activities in this chapter alternate between helping students understand the equivalence of rational numbers and helping them gain fluency and facility in identifying equivalent rational-number expressions. Chapter 2 continues to emphasize helping students build fluency and facility with fractions, decimals, and percents on a foundation of conceptual understanding and sense making. Chapter 2 also extends the study of rational numbers from identifying "equivalent," "greater than," or "less than" to creating algorithms for the operations of addition, subtraction, multiplication, and division.

NAVIGATING *through* NUMBER *and* OPERATIONS

Chapter 2
Working with Fractions, Decimals, and Percents

"Numbers are ideas— abstractions that apply to a broad range of real and imagined situations. Operations on numbers, such as addition and subtraction, are also abstractions. Yet in order to communicate about numbers and operations, people need representations—something physical, spoken, or written. And in order to carry out any of these operations, they need algorithms: step-by- step procedures for computation."

(Kilpatrick, Swafford, and Findell 2001, p. 72)

Important Mathematical Ideas

Chapter 2 features sample activities that can help students in the middle grades develop a conceptual understanding of, and facility and fluency with, rational numbers. The activities encourage mathematical thinking and incorporate hands-on mathematical investigations. These activities are designed to—

- build on students' prior understanding of whole numbers;
- help students develop meaningful representations (physical, numerical, and verbal) of concepts and operations;
- support students' success in solving complex problems;
- promote inquiry and student-invented generalizations and algorithms;
- lay the groundwork for students' understanding of related and more complex mathematical concepts and operations.

In the middle grades, students need regular opportunities to examine their own and one another's thinking, conjectures, and generalizations about important mathematical ideas. The development of computational algorithms—a process that both requires and fosters deep understanding of the meanings of the four basic operations—encourages the generalization and invention that are fundamental to "doing mathematics." The activities in this chapter help students explore how real-life or mathematical contexts—as well as what makes sense in them—affect the reasonableness or usefulness of certain meanings associated with an operation or certain algorithms for carrying out an operation. In the middle grades, students should also encounter strategies and ideas that might not otherwise surface, develop metacognitive and other high-level thinking skills, deepen their understanding of key mathematical concepts and relationships, and develop facility and fluency in problem solving and computation.

When your students struggle in learning situations involving operations and algorithms with rational numbers, consider these questions and how the answers can help you tailor your instruction:

- Do the students understand the meanings of a decimal, fraction, or percent?
- Do they understand the meanings of the basic operations and the relevant contexts in which different meanings apply?
- Has their prior learning centered on hands-on experiences that emphasize communication of their reasoning, thinking, and understanding?
- Do the students use algorithms with understanding?
- Have they had opportunities to invent algorithms, to reason conceptually about algorithms produced by others, and to consider contexts in which one algorithm may be more useful than another?

Algorithms are sets of step-by-step procedures for completing a calculation. As you plan your instruction and work to foster your students' generalization of computation patterns and their creation of algorithms, remember that people have always used a range of resources to carry out algorithms. Such resources include pencil and paper, abacuses, slide rules, fingers, calculators, computers, and other tools. Which tool makes the most sense to use? A number of factors influence the selection, including (a) the depth of understanding of the mathematics related to the calculation, (b) the complexity of the calculation, (c) the speed with which an answer is needed, and (d) the familiarity with the tools available. Kilpatrick, Swafford, and Findell (2001) highlight findings that suggest that one's choice of algorithm is guided by the *transparency*, *efficiency*, *generality*, *precision*, and *simplicity* of the algorithm:

> The more transparent an algorithm, the easier it is to understand, and a child who understands an algorithm can reconstruct it after months or even years of not using it. The need for efficiency depends, of course, on how often an algorithm is used. An additional desired characteristic is *simplicity* because simple algorithms are easier to remember and easier to perform accurately. Again, the key is finding an appropriate balance among these characteristics because, for example, algorithms that are sufficiently general and efficient are not very transparent. It is worth noting that pushing buttons on a calculator is the epitome of a nontransparent algorithm, but it can be quite efficient (p. 103).

"In the middle grades, students should continue to refine their understandings of addition, subtraction, multiplication, and division as they use these operations with fractions, decimals, percents, and integers."
(NCTM 2000, p. 218)

"Teachers need to be attentive to conceptual obstacles that many students encounter as they make the transition from operations with whole numbers [to operations with fractions, decimals, percents, and integers]."
(NCTM 2000, p. 218)

The Meanings of Addition, Multiplication, Subtraction, and Division

Students' knowledge of and facility with the four basic operations comes significantly into play throughout this chapter, and you will be assessing your students' understanding of these operations. Furthermore, you will need to guide them through activities that encourage them to think deeply about computational algorithms and other situations with rational numbers. To receive the most benefit from the activities in this chapter, your students might need additional experiences with the four operations and their meanings. The following background information and examples of students' work should help you in assessing, supporting, and planning for your students' experiences with computations with rational numbers. This discussion of the meanings of the four basic operations uses representations that build on those that students typically use with whole numbers prior to grade 6.

Addition

Students' early notions about the meanings of addition of whole numbers arise from the need to simplify counting in contexts that involve (a) joining together sets of like objects and (b) joining together segments of varied lengths. As shown in figure 2.1, extending these approaches to addition from whole numbers to rational numbers and integers is straightforward. Students just need to recognize that instead of joining whole sets, whole objects, or whole lengths, they are joining parts of sets, objects, or lengths (as long as the objects or units are like), or joining sets with positive and negative values. Conceptually, joining the parts and values makes sense. However, determining the total amount, or value, when working with rational numbers is more complex. Thus, students encounter the need to invent or learn strategies for finding that total.

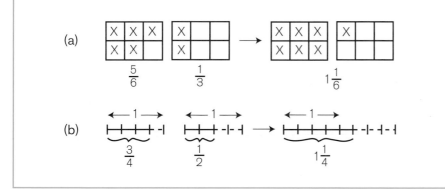

Fig. 2.1.

Addition as joining together (a) sets of like objects or units and (b) segments of varied lengths

Multiplication

One way to represent multiplication is as *repeated addition*. Multiplication involves either joining together repeated segments of the same length and determining the length of the resulting segment or joining together copies of a set of objects. Figure 2.2 shows how the multiplication $4\frac{1}{2} \times 3$ can be viewed as adding together $4\frac{1}{2}$ groups of three square tiles to determine the total number of tiles ($13\frac{1}{2}$). Another way (not pictured) would be combining three groups of $4\frac{1}{2}$ tiles.

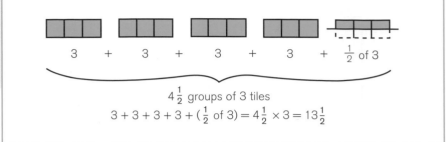

$$3 \quad + \quad 3 \quad + \quad 3 \quad + \quad 3 \quad + \quad \tfrac{1}{2} \text{ of } 3$$

$4\frac{1}{2}$ groups of 3 tiles

$$3 + 3 + 3 + 3 + (\tfrac{1}{2} \text{ of } 3) = 4\tfrac{1}{2} \times 3 = 13\tfrac{1}{2}$$

Notice that the tiles in figure 2.2 can be rearranged to form a *rectangular array* of $4\frac{1}{2} \times 3$ ($4\frac{1}{2}$ rows of 3 tiles, or 3 columns of $4\frac{1}{2}$ tiles). Assuming that one square tile equals one area unit and has an edge length of one linear unit, we can push the tiles in the rectangular array together to form a rectangle whose sides are $4\frac{1}{2}$ linear units and 3 linear units (as in fig. 2.3). This process gives an area representation of $4\frac{1}{2} \times 3$.

Fig. **2.3**.

Multiplication represented as (a) a rectangular array or (b) the area of a rectangle

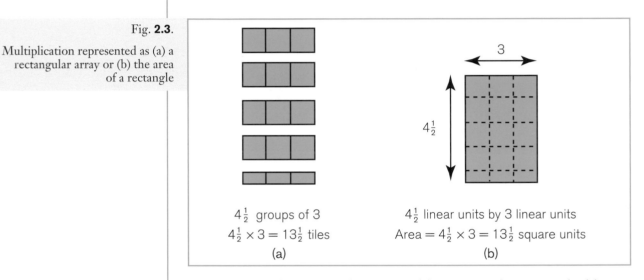

$4\frac{1}{2}$ groups of 3

$4\frac{1}{2} \times 3 = 13\frac{1}{2}$ tiles

(a)

$4\frac{1}{2}$ linear units by 3 linear units

Area $= 4\frac{1}{2} \times 3 = 13\frac{1}{2}$ square units

(b)

Also notice that although it is possible to "see" the repeated addition and the rectangular array of $4\frac{1}{2} \times 3$ in the area representation, the area representation is conceptually quite different. The factors $4\frac{1}{2}$ and 3 do not indicate the number of sets of tiles or the size of a set; rather, those factors are lengths, measured in linear units. The product is the area of the rectangle, measured in square units. As shown in figure 2.4, rotating the rectangle (or the array) illustrates the *commutative property of multiplication*—that the order in which two numbers are multiplied does not affect their product. The area and array representations can also illustrate the *distributive property of multiplication over addition*—that multiplying a sum of two numbers by a third number gives the same answer whether one first finds the sum and then multiplies or first multiplies by each number and then adds the two products.

Another way to view multiplication is as a *Cartesian product*. This representation, which figure 2.5 illlustrates for the product 2×5, is especially useful in probability contexts. As a Cartesian product, 2×5 represents the number of ways in which two objects from one set can be paired with five objects from another set. Figure 2.5b, which shows how an array can represent 2×5 as a Cartesian product, extends the connections among the representations of multiplication. (Note, however,

The commutative property of multiplication states that $ab = ba$ for all real numbers a and b. The distributive property of multiplication over addition states that $a(b + c) = ab + ac$ for all real numbers a, b, and c.

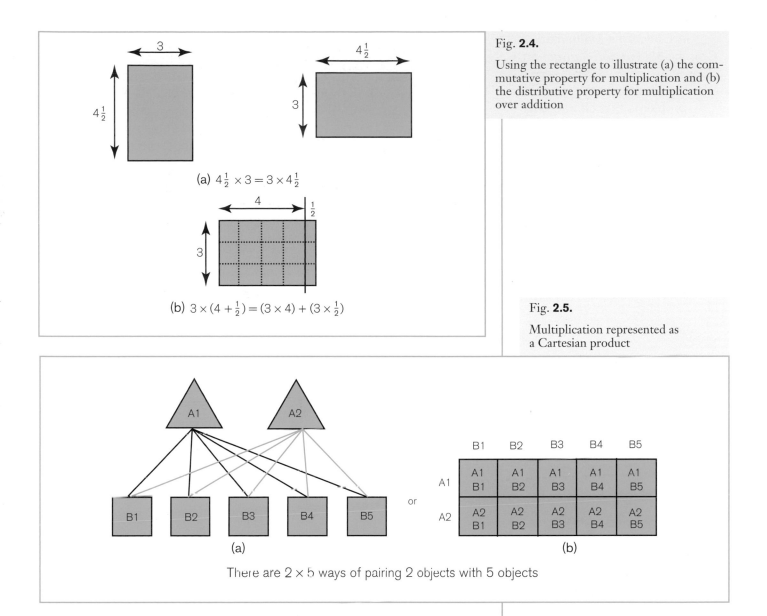

Fig. **2.4.**

Using the rectangle to illustrate (a) the commutative property for multiplication and (b) the distributive property for multiplication over addition

(a) $4\frac{1}{2} \times 3 = 3 \times 4\frac{1}{2}$

(b) $3 \times (4 + \frac{1}{2}) = (3 \times 4) + (3 \times \frac{1}{2})$

Fig. **2.5.**

Multiplication represented as a Cartesian product

(a)   or   (b)

There are 2×5 ways of pairing 2 objects with 5 objects

that the idea of a Cartesian product applies only to whole numbers; pairing $4\frac{1}{2}$ objects with 5 objects, for example, would not make sense.)

Although these ways of thinking about multiplication (repeated addition, rectangular array, area representation, and Cartesian product) are related, they should be considered as separate, context-based *meanings of multiplication*. As students begin multiplying with rational numbers, they are also likely to struggle with how to adapt counting strategies for whole numbers to operations with rational numbers. For example, students may be accustomed to interpreting and solving 3×5 by "adding together three groups of five units." However, they might encounter difficulty in applying repeated addition to compute $\frac{3}{4} \times \frac{5}{6}$ by "adding together $\frac{3}{4}$ of a group of $\frac{5}{6}$ units" or to compute $2\frac{1}{2} \times 3\frac{1}{3}$ by "adding together $2\frac{1}{2}$ rows of $3\frac{1}{3}$ objects." Middle-grades students will also struggle if they harbor the common misconception that multiplication "makes bigger." They might need help recognizing that, with rational numbers, multiplication no longer necessarily produces a number that is larger than one or both of the factors.

In *Children's Mathematics: Cognitively Guided Instruction*, Carpenter et al. (1999) offer a detailed analysis of the types of problems that characterize addition and subtraction situations.

Subtraction

Figure 2.6 illustrates two ways to think about subtraction—take-away and comparison (or difference). As with any operation, students should realize that the way to think about subtraction often depends on the everyday or mathematical context. For example, a context involving two lampposts of heights $14\frac{3}{4}$ feet and $9\frac{1}{2}$ feet prompts a comparison of the difference between the heights of the lampposts (taking away the height of one lamppost from that of the other does not make literal sense). However, a situation involving a full $14\frac{3}{4}$-gallon fuel tank that leaks $9\frac{1}{2}$ gallons prompts an interpretation of subtraction as take-away. Subtraction can also be thought of in relation to addition. The difference between the heights of the lampposts is the amount that must be added to the lamppost that is $9\frac{1}{2}$ feet to make it reach $14\frac{3}{4}$ feet. Likewise, the difference in the amount of fuel can be thought of as the amount of fuel needed to fill a $14\frac{3}{4}$-gallon fuel tank that currently contains $5\frac{1}{4}$ gallons of fuel.

Fig. **2.6.**

Subtraction represented as (a) take-away and (b) comparison (difference)

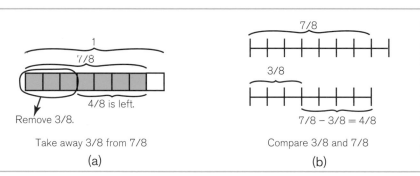

Take away 3/8 from 7/8

(a)

Compare 3/8 and 7/8

(b)

For a detailed analysis of the ways of thinking about the division of fractions, see Sinicrope, Mick, and Kolb (2002; available on the CD-ROM).

Division

The ways of thinking about division are closely related to the ways of thinking about multiplication. If students think of $a \times b = c$ as a multiplication situation in which a and b are nonzero rational numbers, then they should come to think of $c \div a$ and $c \div b$ as related division situations. Several ways exist to think about division. *Sharing* (also called *partitioning*) involves determining the size of a group for a particular number of groups. *Grouping* (also called *measurement* or *repeated subtraction*) involves determining the number of groups of a particular size. Both ways are shown in figure 2.7.

A third way of thinking about division is to think of the quotient as the unknown length of a side of a rectangle whose area and other side are known. In figure 2.8, for example, an area of 6.4 square units is arranged in a rectangular array with dimensions 4 and (6.4 ÷ 4), or 1.6, linear units.

Fig. **2.7.**

Division represented as (a) sharing and (b) as grouping

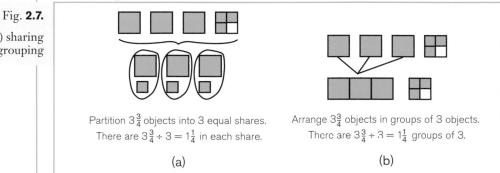

Partition $3\frac{3}{4}$ objects into 3 equal shares. There are $3\frac{3}{4} \div 3 = 1\frac{1}{4}$ in each share.

Arrange $3\frac{3}{4}$ objects in groups of 3 objects. There are $3\frac{3}{4} \div 3 = 1\frac{1}{4}$ groups of 3.

(a)

(b)

Notice that these three meanings of (or ways of thinking about) division build on students' ability to reverse the repeated addition, rectangular array, and area representations for multiplication. When students have mastered reversibility in their thinking, they are not merely working backward through the steps of an algorithm. Rather, they are finding an alternate path for meeting the conditions of the problem (Rachlin 1998; available on the CD-ROM).

For certain computations with rational numbers, some ways of thinking about division might make more sense to students than others. Ultimately, the opportunities students have to make sense of the division of fractions will lead to their creating algorithms that are meaningful to them.

Warrington (1997; available on the CD-ROM) recounts a series of lessons that she conducted to help students make sense of the division of fractions. In one lesson, she gave her fifth- and sixth-grade students the following problem: "I purchased $5\frac{3}{4}$ pounds of chocolate-covered peanuts. I want to store the candy in half-pound bags so that I can freeze it and use it in smaller portions. How many half-pound bags can I make?" One student responded, "Eleven bags, and you would have a quarter of a pound left over, or half a bag." When asked how she obtained that answer, the student replied, "You get ten bags from the five pounds because 5 divided by $\frac{1}{2}$ is 10, and then you get another bag from the $\frac{3}{4}$, which makes eleven bags, and there is one-fourth of a pound left over, which makes half of a half-pound bag."

Another student in the class responded, "I just doubled it $\left[5\frac{3}{4}\right]$ and divided by 1." That student explained that the answer remains the same when both the dividend and the divisor are doubled, as in $10 \div 5 = 2$ and $20 \div 10 = 2$. Determining a unit rate adds another meaning for the division of fractions.

Had Warrington selected another problem with a different context, her students would probably have approached the problem differently. Consider this problem: "Maria has $8\frac{3}{4}$ yards of ribbon that must be cut into sections of $2\frac{1}{4}$ yards each to make bows. How many bows can she make?" In this scenario, the students would probably find it relatively easy to think of finding the number of groups with $2\frac{1}{4}$ yards as the size of each group. They might suggest that they could cut three (almost 4) sections of $2\frac{1}{4}$ yards from the $8\frac{3}{4}$ yards of ribbon. As a follow-up question, the teacher might ask, "What part of a $2\frac{1}{4}$-yard section is left over?" Here the context of the problem might help students think of the division as a repeated subtraction (measurement). In fact, the students might not even realize that the problem involves division. Without the context, they could still think of the computation of $8\frac{3}{4} \div 2\frac{1}{4}$ as grouping—they could "see" and solve the computation, as in figure 2.9.

Students might also think of computing $8\frac{3}{4} \div 2\frac{1}{4}$ as partitioning (sharing). In this situation, shown in figure 2.10, they would try to partition $8\frac{3}{4}$ units evenly into $2\frac{1}{4}$ groups. To make the shares even, they might think of $2\frac{1}{4}$ whole groups as $4 + 4 + 1$, or 9, quarter groups. Then they would need to partition the $8\frac{3}{4}$ units among the 9 quarter groups. Since they could not give each of the quarter groups a whole unit, they could think of the $8\frac{3}{4}$ units as $4 + 4 + 4 + 4 + 4 + 4 + 4 + 4 + 3$, or 35 quarter units. Then they could give each of the 9 quarter groups

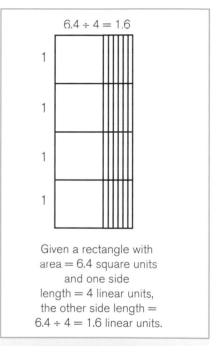

$$6.4 \div 4 = 1.6$$

Given a rectangle with area = 6.4 square units and one side length = 4 linear units, the other side length = $6.4 \div 4 = 1.6$ linear units.

Fig. **2.8.**

Division as the process of finding the unknown side of a rectangle whose area and other side are known

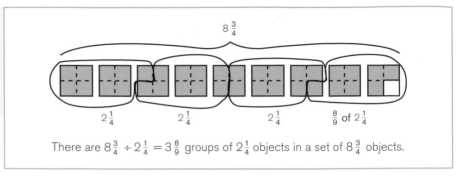

There are $8\frac{3}{4} \div 2\frac{1}{4} = 3\frac{8}{9}$ groups of $2\frac{1}{4}$ objects in a set of $8\frac{3}{4}$ objects.

3 quarter units. They would then have shared 9×3, or 27, quarter units, so they would have 8 quarter units left to share among the 9 quarter groups. To continue the sharing, they could split each of the remaining 8 quarter units into ninths. Then they would be able to share an additional $\frac{8}{9}$ of a quarter-unit with the 9 quarter groups. In total, each of the 9 quarter groups would get $3\frac{8}{9}$ quarter units, so $8\frac{3}{4} \div 2\frac{1}{4} = 3\frac{8}{9}$.

This overview of basic operations with rational numbers should help you identify and support your students' thinking. You can use the discussion and samples included here to create preliminary or follow-up activities or simply to enrich your own background as your students work through the subsequent activities in this chapter.

Laying Conceptual Groundwork for Solving More Complex Problems

As you shift the instructional emphasis from operations on whole numbers to operations on integers and rational numbers, you will probably notice that certain computations prove more relevant and useful for mathematical purposes than for everyday situations. Although learning to understand and carry out such computations might not appear to be especially useful in real-life situations, such skills do give students access to important mathematical concepts and procedures. Students will need facility with these concepts and procedures later in the mathematics curriculum and for future, more complex applications in everyday life. For example, although students might be able to apply division of fractions (e.g., 3/8 ÷ 2/3) to only a few everyday contexts, learning to divide such fractions is fundamental to solving problems involving rational expressions in algebra. Thus, linking representations for division of whole numbers to representations for division of fractions facilitates students' invention of algorithms for dividing fractions, and ultimately, for completing algebraic operations.

What Might Students Already Know about These Ideas?

From prekindergarten through grade 5, students' work with number emphasizes concepts of and operations with whole numbers. However, during the elementary grades, students also encounter situations that foster intuitions about a broader system of numbers and that set the stage for exploring integers and rational numbers in the middle grades. For example, students will have encountered such situations as computing a score on a board game after winning ten points and losing fifteen

One way the students can divide $8\frac{3}{4}$ by $2\frac{1}{4}$ is to try to share $8\frac{3}{4}$ units among $2\frac{1}{4}$ groups.

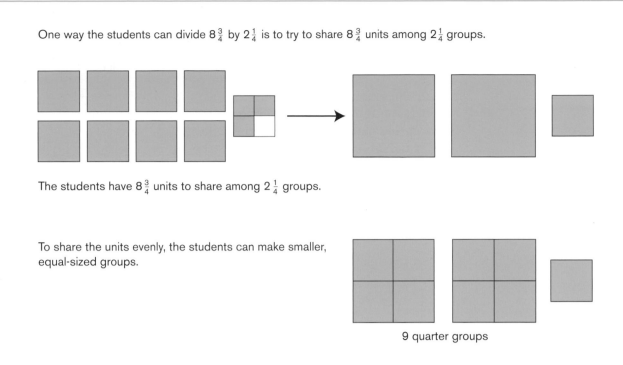

The students have $8\frac{3}{4}$ units to share among $2\frac{1}{4}$ groups.

To share the units evenly, the students can make smaller, equal-sized groups.

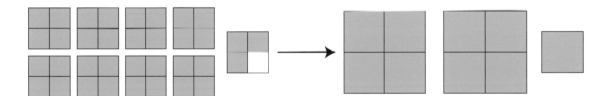

9 quarter groups

Since the students cannot give each of the 9 quarter groups 1 whole unit, they should divide the units to share them. Suppose they divide them into quarter units:

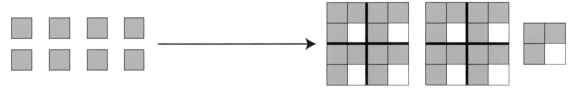

Then the students can give each of the 9 quarter groups 3 quarter units.

Now the students still have 8 quarters to share among the 9 quarter groups.

To share the 8 quarter units evenly among the 9 quarter groups, the students will need to divide them into ninths and give each group $\frac{8}{9}$ of a quarter unit. So, in all, each quarter group will get $3\frac{8}{9}$ quarter units.

Fig. **2.10.**

Finding the quotient of $8\frac{3}{4}$ and $2\frac{1}{4}$ by partitioning (sharing) points, or figuring out how much candy each of three people receives if they share two candy bars equally. Such experiences in the elementary grades with whole-number operations that do not produce whole-number results provide a meaningful starting point for developing middle-grades students' understanding of integers and rational numbers and the operations involving integers and rational numbers. This grounding increases the students' likelihood of meaningful generalization, invention, and new learning about those ideas.

Students entering the middle grades—especially those who have previously encountered curricula aligned with *Principles and Standards for School Mathematics* (NCTM 2000)—are likely to have had extensive hands-on, conceptually-focused experiences that emphasized the following:

- Generating and recognizing equivalent forms of simple fractions, decimals, and percents
- Using fractions as measures, quantities, parts of a whole, locations on a number line, and indicated divisions
- Ordering and comparing fractions between 0 and 1 in relation to benchmarks such as 0, 1/4, 1/2, 3/4, and 1
- Reasoning about operations on numbers (e.g., explaining that 1/3 + 1/4 must be less than 1 because each addend is less than 1/2)
- Exploring the meanings of the arithmetic operations

The first activity in chapter 2, Thinking about Mathematical Ideas, helps students consciously extend their prior knowledge and experience with operations on whole numbers to support their development of algorithms for comparable operations with rational numbers. The activity also gives you an opportunity to assess your students' knowledge of and facility with these concepts before you move on to the increasingly complex explorations later in this chapter.

Thinking about Mathematical Ideas

Goals

- Assess students' background in, and depth of understanding of, the meanings of the four basic operations (addition, subtraction, multiplication, and division)
- Foster students' reflection about, interaction with, and understanding of concepts and operations related to rational numbers

Materials

For each student—

- A copy of the blackline master "Thinking about Mathematical Ideas"

For the students to use as needed—

- Cubes, tiles, scissors, grid paper, and number strips
- Blank transparency sheets and markers (optional)

For the teacher—

- An overhead projector (optional)

p. 121

Activity

Place the students in small groups. Distribute a copy of the blackline master "Thinking about Mathematical Ideas" to each student. The activity sheet allows you to give your students a specific mathematical idea and have them explain its meaning, illustrate it in diagrams and mathematical problems, explore multiple solution methods, and pose any questions that they have about the idea. Ask the students to fill in the blank after "Mathematical Idea" with the phrase "addition of whole numbers, fractions, and decimals." Have the students work individually to complete question 1, which asks them to explain the idea's meaning. Tell the students that they are free to use grid paper and other manipulatives to help them think through their answers, and be sure to have these resources handy for the students to use.

Your students may want grid paper for this activity. A reproducible template for centimeter grid paper appears on page 134.

Next, have the students take turns presenting their answers in their small groups. Circulate and listen to their discussions to gain a sense of their understanding and thought processes. After the reports, encourage the small groups or the whole class to discuss and debate the ideas. Follow the same process for questions 2–5 on the activity sheet. To help you plan future instruction, collect and review the students' written responses.

Each time you start instruction on one of the other rational number operations (subtraction, multiplication, and division), repeat this activity with the focus on the current mathematical idea. This activity should continue to help you with planning, and it will help the students expand their thinking in preparation for further experiences.

Discussion

The students' responses should offer insight into their background knowledge and the extent to which their thinking is grounded in conceptual understanding as opposed to rote memorization of facts and routines. Throughout the activity, be sure to provide plenty of time for students to work individually before they discuss their ideas in the small groups and with the whole class.

This activity should help you introduce instruction for applying each of the four basic operations to rational numbers. See the introduction to this chapter for an overview of those operations. This overview delves into what these operations mean and the ways that students can approach them conceptually. It also explains ways that students can extend what they already know about operations with whole numbers to operations with rational numbers.

During the class discussion of the activity, invite student volunteers to use diagrams or models to demonstrate their thinking on an overhead projector or at the board. It might be helpful to post some of the students' illustrations of the key representations in the classroom. Both you and the students can refer to this list for reference and refinement as instruction proceeds. If the students' ideas are redundant or incomplete, you can either have the class discuss how to consolidate, revise, or extend the list during the current discussion, or have the class revisit and revise the list during upcoming lessons.

To help you plan your instruction, monitor the students' discussions as well as their written responses for evidence that they understand the meanings and mathematical representations of the numbers and the operations. Also look for evidence that they are making connections across representations. For example, do the students move easily from one representation to another? As you extend instruction to other operations, do the students' verbal, visual (or concrete), symbolic, and everyday representations suggest a coherent view of each operation and of the relationships among the operations? Where are the gaps in their understanding? Do the students' computations appear to be based on understanding or on rote procedures that lack meaning to them? Determine what other information about the students' thinking would help your instructional planning, and use this activity to try to gather it.

Selected Instructional Activities

It might be helpful for you to save the students' written responses to the activity Thinking about Mathematical Ideas and then reassign the activity after you have completed new instruction on concepts of and operations with rational numbers. Compare, or have the students compare, their "before" and "after" responses for evidence of growth. If the students keep journals, you might ask them to record all their responses to this activity in their journals. Periodically, have them look back at their responses, refine their thinking, and self-assess how and why their thinking is developing. Since students' responses should grow in depth and sophistication in grades 6–8, the responses might make useful entries in a portfolio that documents the students' mathematical development in the middle grades.

The activity Thinking about Mathematical Ideas helps you gather background information to guide your implementation of activities focused on new learning. The next four activities—Linden's Algorithm, Linden's Algorithm Revisited, Erica's Algorithm, and Keonna's Conjecture—form a series on investigating algorithms. The activities successively build on the drawings, sketches, or models that students use to illustrate their thinking about operations on rational numbers. All four activities are designed to deepen students' mathematical understanding, foster productive mathematical habits of mind, and facilitate fluency with operations involving rational numbers. The chapter's concluding activity, Fraction Situations, helps students analyze number situations and gives them opportunities to pose and solve problems.

Linden's Algorithm

Goals

- Analyze and invent computational algorithms that are based on conceptual models and strategies
- Reason about the relevance and application of various visual representations and computational algorithms to everyday life and mathematical contexts
- Use the area model for multiplication as a context for generalizing about relationships among whole numbers, fractions, and decimal fractions
- Recognize the role and usefulness of the distributive property in carrying out fraction computations

Materials

For each student—

- A copy of the blackline master "Linden's Algorithm"

For the students to use as needed—

- A variety of materials (tiles, grid paper, egg cartons, fraction bars, base-ten pieces, etc.)

For the teacher—

- An overhead projector (optional)
- A transparency of "Linden's Algorithm—Diagrams" (optional; available on the CD-ROM)

pp. 122–24

Activity

Display "2/3 × 4/5" on an overhead projector or the board. Ask the students to work individually to make one or more diagrams, sketches, or models to illustrate what they think 2/3 × 4/5 means and to show a visual strategy for determining the product. Ask the students to describe an everyday situation that they could represent by each diagram or model. Arrange the students in pairs to discuss their ideas, refine their thinking, clarify their questions, and identify challenging ideas. Then discuss the students' models and strategies as a large group and invite several volunteers to show their thinking on an overhead projector or the board.

Next, distribute a copy of the activity sheet "Linden's Algorithm" to each student. The worksheet presents a journal entry by a student named Linden, who successfully extended the area representation for the multiplication of whole numbers to the multiplication of fractions (see the margin). Have the students work with their partners to study Linden's statements and drawings and complete questions 1 and 2, which ask them what step-by-step procedures Linden used to find the product and whether they can adapt Linden's method to the products of other fractions. Have the class discuss the students' ideas, examples, and arguments. Volunteers can show their reasoning by using a

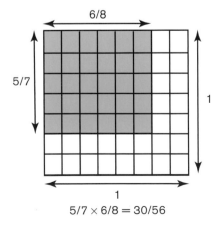

5/7 × 6/8 = 30/56

transparency of "Linden's Algorithms—Diagrams" on an overhead projector or by working on the board.

After the class discussion, you should have a good idea of the students' level of understanding and which areas they need to explore further. Use this information to tailor the rest of the activity to your students' needs. If you want, you can assign some of the remaining questions on the activity sheet for investigation by pairs of students and use other questions for class discussion. Additional questions and problems that you might pose to the students include the following:

- "Recall your own and your classmates' visual methods of solving $2/3 \times 4/5$. Were they similar to or different from Linden's? Invent algorithms that represent the computations in those visual methods."

- "Do those methods generalize (work for all fraction products)?"

- "Are there other fraction and decimal multiplication ideas that surprise or confuse you or that you wonder about? If so, what are they?"

Discussion

The students should have had a range of hands-on experiences to discover the meanings of the basic operations and the meanings of fractions and decimals. Be sure to have materials and manipulatives (such as tiles, grid paper, egg cartons, fraction bars, base-ten pieces, and so on) readily accessible to students as they complete this activity.

As you begin the activity, note that the students might use a range of visual strategies for computing $2/3 \times 4/5$. Figure 2.11 illustrates two examples based on different representations of the meaning of multiplication. One applies the computation to ordering pizzas for a party and uses the repeated addition representation of multiplication. The other shows the computation as an area representation.

Listen to the students' ideas for clues about their understanding and needs. Do the students think about the meaning of $2/3 \times 4/5$ according to the repeated addition, array, or area representation of multiplication? Do they recognize that different meanings suggest different visual strategies? Does everyday context influence their interpretation of meaning or choice of strategy? Are there methods that some students use repeatedly on certain types of problems or all products of fractions?

Questions 3 and 4 on the activity sheet and the additional questions listed above give you options for fostering the students' understanding of and ability to articulate the fundamental mathematical ideas behind the area representation and multiplying fractions. Some of these options could launch an investigation that spans several hours of class time; others might require much less time. Use the students' level of engagement and learning needs, along with your overall instructional goals, to determine the options you pursue and the time you allot for them.

Consider whether a given activity might deepen students' understanding, raise contradictions that could lead to insights, or lay groundwork for future mathematical work. For example, question 4(*a*) probes Linden's surprise to see that the product of two fractions could be smaller than either fraction. The students must explain how Linden's area representation of $5/7 \times 6/8$ shows that $30/56$ is smaller than both

Mario ordered five pizzas for his party—one for each table. He ordered 4/5 of the pizzas with extra cheese,

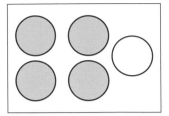

and he wanted 2/3 of each pizza to have pepperoni.

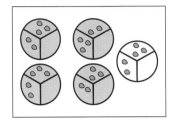

Of the thirds of a pizza, 8 have pepperoni and extra cheese. 8/15 of the total order has pepperoni and extra cheese.

$$\frac{2}{3} \times \frac{4}{5} = \left(\frac{2}{3} \times 4 \right) \times \frac{1}{5} = \frac{8}{15}$$

(a)

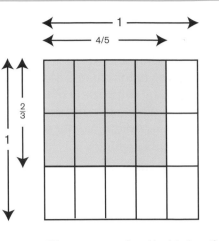

Given a rectangle with side lengths 2/3 and 4/5 linear units, the area is 2/3 x 4/5 = 8/15 square units.

(b)

Fig. 2.11.

Two visual strategies, (a) repeated addition and (b) area representation, for multiplying 2/3 and 4/5 (2/3 × 4/5 = 8/15)

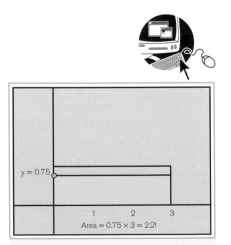

Fig. 2.12.

A sample screen from the applet Learning about Multiplication (figure does not show applet's actual colors)

5/7 and 6/8. Some students might state that they can "see" that Linden's 5/7 × 6/8 rectangle covers less area than either a 5/7 × 1 or a 6/8 × 1 rectangle. Therefore, they might say that 5/7 × 6/8 is less than either 5/7 or 6/8. Other students might argue that, according to the repeated addition representation, 5/7 × 6/8 represents 5/7 of a group of 6/8, which is only a *portion* of 6/8. Hence they would say that 5/7 × 6/8 must be less than 6/8. Similarly, on the basis of the commutative property for multiplication, they could view 5/7 × 6/8 as 6/8 of a group of 5/7; hence, 5/7 × 6/8 must also be less than 5/7. Through other examples and similar reasoning, students should be able to see that for any product, whenever a factor is a fraction between 0 and 1, the product is less than the other factor.

The applet Learning about Multiplication on the CD-ROM offers a dynamic area representation for multiplying a range of decimal numbers from 0 to 3 by the fixed number 3. In figure 2.12, a screen from the applet shows that the area of a rectangle with sides 0.75 and 3 is less than the area of a 1 × 3 unit rectangle. By dragging the dot on the vertical axis, students can see that this relation is true for all lengths between 0 and 1.

In Linden's Algorithm, students draw on their knowledge of the area representation of multiplication of whole numbers. They apply and expand what they know to develop algorithms to multiply fractions. In the next activity, Linden's Algorithm Revisited, they continue this process by exploring the area representation, the distributive property, and algorithms for decimals and binomials.

Linden's Algorithm Revisited

Goals

- Extend experiences in multiplying fractions from Linden's Algorithm to explore using the area model for multiplication as a context for generalizing about relationships among whole numbers, fractions, decimal fractions, and binomials
- Analyze and invent computational algorithms that are based on conceptual models and strategies
- Reason about the relevance and application of various visual representations and computational algorithms to mathematical contexts
- Recognize the role and usefulness of the distributive property in moving from an area model for multiplication to carrying out fraction computations

Materials

For each student—

- A copy of the blackline master "Linden's Algorithm Revisited"

For the students to use as needed—

- A variety of materials (e.g., tiles, grid paper, egg cartons, fraction bars, base-ten pieces, etc.)

For the teacher—

- An overhead projector (optional)
- A transparency of "Linden's Algorithm Revisited—Diagrams" (optional; available on the CD-ROM)

pp. 125–26

Activity

Before starting this activity, the students should have completed the previous activity sheet, "Linden's Algorithm." Distribute a copy of the new activity sheet, "Linden's Algorithm Revisited," to each student. Here Linden uses her area representation to compute 14×23, 1.4×2.3, and $(x + 4)(2x + 3)$. (See figure 2.13.) Have the students work in pairs to complete question 1, which asks them to complete and explain diagrams like those in the figure for the three computations. Then ask for volunteers to share their ideas on the board or on a transparency of "Linden's Algorithm Revisited—Diagrams."

Next, ask the students to work with their partners to complete questions 2 and 3 on the activity sheet. For question 2, the students

Fig. 2.13.

Linden's area representation for 14×23, 1.4×2.3, and $(x + 4)(2x + 3)$

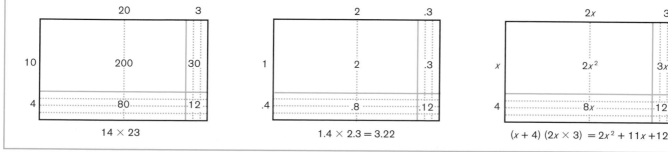

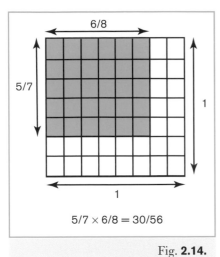

Fig. 2.14.

Linden's visual method for using an area representation of multiplication to find the products of whole numbers and fractions

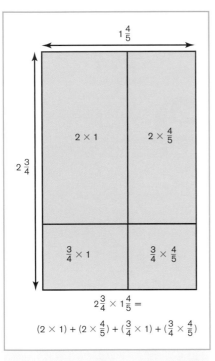

Fig. 2.15.

Using an area representation to multiply $2\frac{3}{4}$ and $1\frac{4}{5}$, which also illustrates the distributive property for multiplication over addition (applied twice)

Fig 2.16.

Using the area of rectangles to illustrate the distributive property for multiplication over addition

need to show how Linden could adjust the visual method that she used in Linden's Algorithm (shown in fig. 2.14) to compute $2\frac{3}{4} \times 1\frac{4}{5}$. When they have completed questions 2 and 3, have them share and discuss the computational algorithms they wrote for question 3.

After the class has discussed the students' answers, you might want to pose these questions and problems to help your students extend their thinking:

- "Linden's three rectangles illustrate the distributive property for multiplication over addition. What are other examples of this property? What other properties facilitate computation?"
- "What other decimal products can you find by using the area representation?"
- "Describe relationships and differences among Linden's representations and among the area and linear representations within each of the three diagrams."
- "Using the area representation of multiplication, invent an algorithm for computing the product of two decimal fractions. Use a diagram or model to show why your algorithm works."

Discussion

As the students work with Linden's diagrams in question 1, they might develop a variety of systems for recording the partial products that they "see" in the rectangles. Thus, they might create a variety of algorithms for computing products of two-digit whole numbers or decimal numbers, mixed numbers, and binomials. This experience also offers a context for the students to discuss the use of the commutative, associative, and distributive properties to simplify calculations. The students should be able to demonstrate whether, how, and why these properties apply to operations involving rational numbers. In question 2, the students can apply Linden's area representation to $2\frac{3}{4} \times 1\frac{4}{5}$, as shown in figure 2.15.

The area representations in this activity provide a very useful illustration of the distributive property of multiplication over addition. When a, b, c, and d are real numbers, any product of the form $(a + b)(c + d)$ can be viewed as the sum of partial products. Figure 2.16 shows two examples of the distributive property as applied to the area of rectangles.

The applet Multiplication of Fractions on the CD-ROM provides a possible concluding task for this activity. The applet can help the students connect an area model for multiplying either proper or improper fractions to an algorithm for multiplying fractions. Figure 2.17 shows

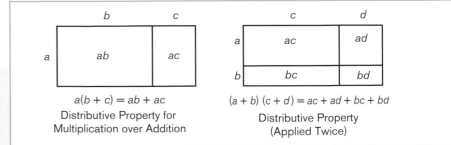

how the applet models the product of 4/3 and 5/4. The shaded regions also give a visual demonstration of the distributive property, showing that 4/3 × 5/4 = (3/3 +1/3) × (4/4 + 1/4) = (3/3 × 4/4) + (3/3 × 1/4) + (1/3 × 4/4) + (1/3 × 1/4).

Area models such as that in the applet Multiplication of Fractions have one instructional drawback. They tend to downplay the unit to which a fraction refers for its meaning, or the fraction's *referent*. When students use an area model, they need to "see" the units that give the fractions their meanings. In figure 2.17, for example, 4/3 designates the portion of the side of the 2 × 2 rectangle that is 4/3 units long. The students should see that 4/3 thus "refers to" one linear unit for meaning, as does 5/4, which designates the portion of the adjacent side of the 2 × 2 rectangle that is 5/4 units long.

The model uses these lengths—4/3 and 5/4 units—to construct the 4/3 × 2 rectangle (the regions shown as gray and dark green in fig. 2.17) and the 2 × 5/4 rectangle (the regions shown as gray and light green) inside the 2 × 2 rectangle. In examining these rectangles, students may see that with the correct referent, 4/3 and 5/4 can designate area as well as length. The area of the 4/3 × 2 rectangle is 4/3 square units when 4/3 refers for meaning to a unit of area that is 1 × 2, or one-half of the area of the 2 × 2 rectangle. Likewise, the area of the 2 × 5/4 rectangle is 5/4 square units when 5/4 refers to one-half of the area of the 2 × 2 rectangle.

The model shows the intersection of the 4/3 × 2 and 2 × 5/4 rectangles as a rectangle whose dimensions are 4/3 × 5/4 (the gray region in fig. 2.17). This rectangle illustrates the product 4/3 × 5/4, or 20/12. But what is this fraction's referent unit? Students should examine the model to see that the product of 5/4 and 4/3, or 20/12, once again

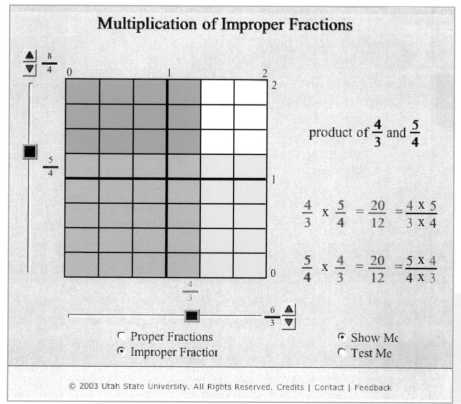

Fig. **2.17.**

Using the Multiplication of Fractions applet to find the product of 4/3 and 5/4 (applet developed by and used with the permission of Utah State University; figure does not show applet's actual colors)

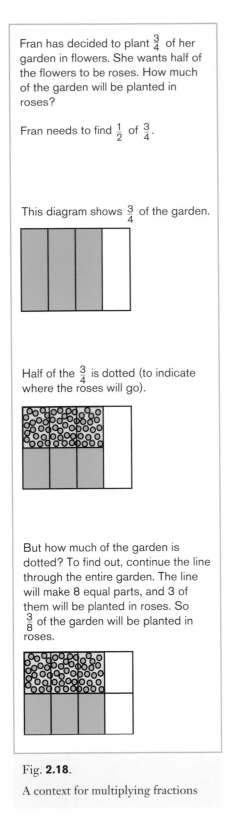

Fran has decided to plant $\frac{3}{4}$ of her garden in flowers. She wants half of the flowers to be roses. How much of the garden will be planted in roses?

Fran needs to find $\frac{1}{2}$ of $\frac{3}{4}$.

This diagram shows $\frac{3}{4}$ of the garden.

Half of the $\frac{3}{4}$ is dotted (to indicate where the roses will go).

But how much of the garden is dotted? To find out, continue the line through the entire garden. The line will make 8 equal parts, and 3 of them will be planted in roses. So $\frac{3}{8}$ of the garden will be planted in roses.

Fig. **2.18**.

A context for multiplying fractions

refers to a portion of the area of the 2×2 rectangle for meaning. However, this time the unit of area is 1×1, or 1 square unit—one-quarter of the area of the 2×2 rectangle instead of one-half of its area.

Placing a multiplication of fractions task in context, such as the garden context provided in figure 2.18, may help you clarify the role of the referent for the students. The garden model uses two referent units (the entire garden and 3/4 of the garden). The students should see that 3/4 refers to the entire garden, 1/2 refers to 3/4 of the garden (not to the entire garden), and 3/8 once again refers to the entire garden as the unit—1/2 of 3/4 of a garden is equivalent to 3/8 of the entire garden.

In the next activity, Erica's Algorithm, students explore a different approach to the area representation. In this instance, they consider the usefulness and appropriateness of enlarging the fractional dimensions of rectangles so that they can work with whole numbers.

Erica's Algorithm

Goals

- Explore and test a different approach to an area representation for multiplying fractions
- Analyze and invent computational algorithms that are based on conceptual models and strategies
- Reason about the relevance and application of various visual representations and computational algorithms to everyday life and mathematical contexts
- Use an area model for multiplication and division as a context for generalizing about relationships among whole numbers, fractions, decimal fractions, and binomials
- Recognize the role and usefulness of the distributive property in carrying out fraction computations

Materials

For each student—

- A copy of the blackline master "Erica's Algorithm"

For the students to use as needed—

- A variety of materials (e.g., tiles, grid paper, egg cartons, fraction bars, base-ten pieces, etc.)

For the teacher—

- An overhead projector (optional)

Activity

Give each student a copy of the blackline master "Erica's Algorithm." Like Linden in the previous activities, Erica uses an area model to multiply fractions, but Erica's approach is different. She draws a rectangle to represent the multiplication and then makes two other, larger rectangles that allow her to think in whole numbers. (See Erica's steps in fig. 2.19.) Place the students in pairs to answer question 1, which asks them to study Erica's visual method and to speculate about the steps she followed. Then discuss their observations as a class. Make sure that the students understand the approach and why it worked.

Next, decide whether you would like to have the students work on questions 2–5 as a class or with their partners. These questions ask the students to apply Erica's method, generalize it, tell whether it is in fact completely different from Linden's, and explain whether or not it will work for mixed numbers and decimals. Discuss your students' answers as needed to solidify and extend their thinking. You might want to select only one or two questions for the students to complete, depending on the time you have and how well they understand the concepts.

Now ask the students to reconsider Linden's algorithm, Erica's algorithm, and other methods or algorithms developed by students in the class. Ask them what contexts (in both everyday life and purely

pp. 127–28

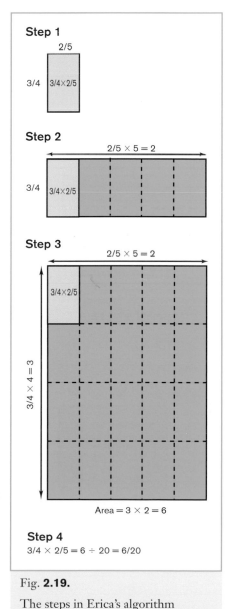

Fig. 2.19.

The steps in Erica's algorithm

numerical situations) might make one approach more efficient, relevant, or accurate than another. Discuss their responses as a large group.

Display the computations 9 ÷ 8 and 3/4 ÷ 1/3 on an overhead projector or the board. Ask the students to make a diagram or sketch that illustrates what they think these computations mean and how they can solve the computations visually on the basis of these meanings. Invite volunteers to demonstrate their diagrams and reasoning in front of the class. Encourage the students to discuss ways in which their methods do or do not generalize. Depending on the time and your students' skill, you might want to pose one or more of the following questions or problems to them:

- "How are the grouping, sharing, and area representations of 9 ÷ 8 and 3/4 ÷ 1/3 similar? How are they different? Explain contexts in which you would think about the problems according to each meaning."
- "Can you adapt Linden's area representation of multiplication to solve 9 ÷ 8 and 3/4 ÷ 1/3?"
- "The fact that a product isn't necessarily larger than its factors surprised Linden. In division, how does the size of the quotient compare to the divisor and dividend? Why? Are these relationships the same or different for fractions, decimals, and whole numbers? Explain."
- "What division relationships surprise or confuse you?"
- "In her approach, Erica changes the area representation of a fraction multiplication problem so that the problem involves whole numbers. Will that method work for the area representation of a fraction division problem? If so, how, and why? If not, why not? What about the division of decimal fractions?"

Discussion

Analyzing algorithms invented by others exposes students to ideas and questions that might not otherwise surface, engages students in critical thinking, and models and motivates students' inventions. For example, analyzing Erica's approach can foster connections and spark other generalizations. Erica's approach involves the synthesis of the following fundamental concepts and relationships:

- The area of a rectangle is the product of the lengths of its sides.
- Given the area of a rectangle and the length of one side, we can find the quotient as the length of the other side.
- One meaning of the fraction a/b is as the quotient, $a ÷ b$, for $b \neq 0$.
- Combining the three previous ideas shows why $a \times (c/a) = c$ (see the illustration in fig. 2.20).

When the length of the side of a rectangle is multiplied (or divided) by a factor, the area is multiplied (or divided) by the same factor (see fig. 2.21). This situation also illustrates *direct variation*; in this case, the area varies directly with the length of a side, and vice versa.

Depending on their prior experience, the students might confuse this relationship with the relationship between the length of the side

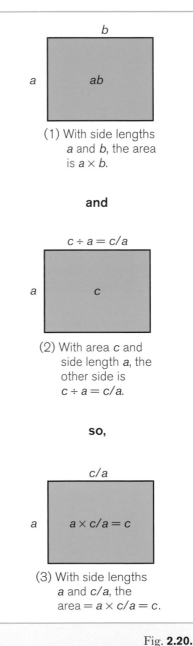

(1) With side lengths a and b, the area is $a \times b$.

and

(2) With area c and side length a, the other side is $c ÷ a = c/a$.

so,

(3) With side lengths a and c/a, the area $= a \times c/a = c$.

Fig. **2.20.**

A graphic demonstration of $a \times (c/a) = c$

Navigating through Number and Operations in Grades 6–8

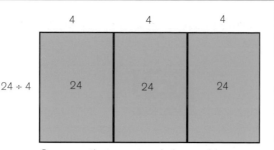

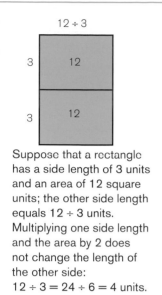

12 ÷ 3

3 | 12

3 | 12

24 ÷ 4

4   4   4

24   24   24

Suppose that a rectangle has a side length of 3 units and an area of 12 square units; the other side length equals 12 ÷ 3 units. Multiplying one side length and the area by 2 does not change the length of the other side:
12 ÷ 3 = 24 ÷ 6 = 4 units.

Suppose that a rectangle has a side length of 4 units and an area of 24 square units; the other side length equals 24 ÷ 4 units. Multiplying one side length and the area by 3 does not change the length of the other side:

24 ÷ 4 = 72 ÷ 12 = 6 units.

Fig. 2.21.

The area of a rectangle varies directly with the length of a side, and vice versa

of a square and the area of the square. In the case of the square, when the side is multiplied (or divided) by a factor, the area is multiplied (or divided) by the square of the same factor; multiplying the length by a given factor forces the width to be multiplied by the same factor for the figure to remain a square. By focusing on this potential confusion, you can help students extend their generalization to what happens to the area of a rectangle when the length is multiplied (or divided) by a factor and the width is multiplied (or divided) by a different factor.

Erica's method generalizes for any product $a/b \times c/d$ (in which b and d are positive integers not equal to zero). Take, for example, a rectangle with dimensions a/b and c/d. Multiplying one dimension by b and the other dimension by d creates a larger rectangle that has an area $a \times c$. That rectangle can be subdivided into $b \times d$ copies of the original rectangle. Hence, the area of the original rectangle is $(a \times c) \div (b \times d)$. The diagram Erica used to generalize her method is shown in figure 2.22. Although this method produces the same algorithm that Linden used (see Linden's Algorithm and Linden's Algorithm Revisited), the reasoning to reach that algorithm is indeed different.

Erica's method can also be adapted to division, as illustrated in figure 2.23. In the area representation of division, the area and one dimension are known. The diagram is used to find the value of the other dimension. Erica's procedure then requires transforming the area and given dimension into whole-number values. The other dimension remains unchanged and equal to the original quotient, but it can now be expressed as the quotient of two whole numbers rather than two fractions.

As an extension to this activity, have the students investigate and generalize about the effect of changing the length of the side of a rectangle in which the area remains fixed. To keep the area fixed, *multiplying* one dimension by a factor requires *dividing* the other side by the same factor. Thus, the lengths of the sides vary inversely and so this example would give a visual representation of *inverse variation*.

The next activity, Keonna's Conjecture, helps students expand their thinking about equal quotients, enabling them to simplify calculations and make generalizations about division.

1. To find the product of $a/b \times c/d$, set up an area representation.

2. Multiply the area and left side by b.

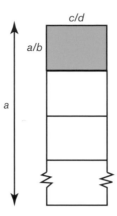

3. Multiply the area and top side by d.

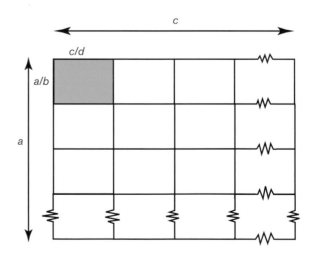

4. The enlarged rectangle gives $b \times d$ copies of the original rectangle. The area of the enlarged rectangle is $a \times c$. The area of the original rectangle is $(a \times c) \div (b \times d)$.

Fig. **2.22.**

Erica's generalization of her method to the area of a rectangle with dimensions a/b and c/d is $(a \times c) \div (b \times d)$

Goal: Use Erica's method to divide 2/3 by 4/5.

Step 1: Make a rectangle with an area of 2/3 square units and one side length of 4/5 units. The other side length is (2/3 ÷ 4/5) units.

4/5

2/3 | 2/3 ÷ 4/5

Step 2: Make the length of the given side of the rectangle a whole number by multiplying the length of the side and the area by 5.

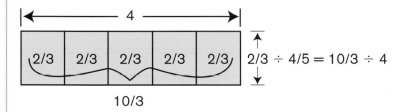

|← ——————— 4 ——————— →|

| 2/3 | 2/3 | 2/3 | 2/3 | 2/3 | 2/3 ÷ 4/5 = 10/3 ÷ 4

10/3

The length of the known side is now 4 units, and the area of the enlarged rectangle is 10/3 square units. Since the length of the other side of the rectangle remains constant, 2/3 ÷ 4/5 = 10/3 ÷ 4.

Step 3: Make the area of the rectangle a whole number by multiplying the area and the length of the known side by 3.

|← ——————————————— 4 × 3 = 12 ——————————————— →|

| 2/3 | 2/3 | 2/3 | 2/3 | 2/3 | 2/3 | 2/3 | 2/3 | 2/3 | 2/3 | 2/3 | 2/3 | 2/3 | 2/3 | 2/3 |

30/3 = 10

The length of the given side of the enlarged rectangle is now 12 units, and the area of the enlarged rectangle is now 10 square units. Since the length of the other side of the rectangle remains constant, its length is 2/3 ÷ 4/5 = 10 ÷ 12.

Step 4: Therefore, we know that 2/3 ÷ 4/5 = 10/12.

Fig. **2.23.**

Applying Erica's algorithm to division for 2/3 ÷ 4/5

Keonna's Conjecture

Goals

- Analyze and test a new conjecture about division of fractions, and evaluate whether it can be generalized to other operations
- Analyze and invent computational algorithms that are based on conceptual models and strategies
- Reason about the relevance and application of various visual representations and computational algorithms to everyday life and mathematical contexts
- Use the area model for multiplication and division as a context for generalizing about relationships among whole numbers, fractions, decimal fractions, and binomials
- Recognize the role and usefulness of the distributive property in carrying out fraction computations

Materials

For each student—

- A copy of the blackline master "Keonna's Conjecture"

For the students to use as needed—

- A variety of materials (e.g., tiles, grid paper, egg cartons, fraction bars, base-ten pieces, etc.)

Activity

Distribute a copy of the blackline master "Keonna's Conjecture" to each student. After making many area representations for the division of fractions, Keonna speculates that she will get the same quotient for $9 \div 8$, $9/10 \div 8/10$, $9/4 \div 8/4$, $9/12 \div 8/12$, and $9/5 \div 8/5$. (See the diagrams in fig. 2.24.) She conjectures that no matter what nonzero number x she uses in $9/x \div 8/x$, the quotient will always be the same. Have the class review Keonna's conjecture. Then ask the students to work individually or in pairs to answer question 1, which asks them to use visual representations to show whether they think Keonna's conjecture is true or false. Invite volunteers to share their diagrams and reasoning with the class, and encourage comments on their ideas. Although they might use different approaches and reasoning, the students should find that Keonna's conjecture is true. The discussion below details some possible approaches.

Next, have the students investigate the other possibilities that Keonna wondered about (questions 2 and 3 on the activity sheet). Does the conjecture hold for other numerators beside 9 and 8? Does it hold for subtraction? For addition? For multiplication? The students should use diagrams and careful reasoning to support their ideas. They should find that Keonna's conjecture holds true for other numerators but not for subtraction, addition, or multiplication. See the discussion below for some examples.

Turn the students' attention next to creating algorithms. On the back of the activity sheet or on another sheet of paper, ask the students to create an algorithm (a complete set of instructions for accomplishing

p. 129

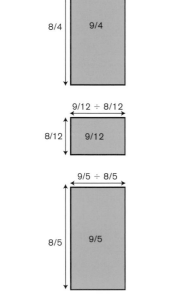

Fig. **2.24.**

Area representations showing that the area varies directly with the length of a side, and vice versa

the task) for dividing fractions. They should explain and show how and why the algorithm works. Remind them to think about the visual methods that they and their classmates have used to divide fractions.

To help the students bring together everything that they have learned in the activities on algorithms in chapter 2, ask them to work with partners to invent algorithms for adding and subtracting fractions. This exercise should help them further generalize the visual strategies that they have been using. It should also help them root their understanding of algorithms in their developing understanding of the meanings of the operations.

Discussion

Your students are likely to use various strategies and rationales to determine whether Keonna's statement is true. Area representations for division provide one possible way—a strategy that also gives you an opportunity to foster students' thinking about equal quotients. In such representations, each quotient—9/10 ÷ 8/10, 9/4 ÷ 8/4, 9/12 ÷ 8/12, and 9/5 ÷ 8/5—represents the length of the side of a rectangle (see fig. 2.24). Using the concept of direct variation that Erica relied on, the students can transform each rectangle into a rectangle with an area of 9 units and side lengths 8 units and 9/8 units. They can do this by multiplying the given areas and left side lengths by the common denominators—10, 4, 12, and 5, respectively.

The students should see that changing the area and one side length of a rectangle by the same factor does not change the length of the other side (the quotient). Therefore, all the quotients must be equal. So, 9/10 ÷ 8/10 = 9/4 ÷ 8/4 = 9/12 ÷ 8/12 = 9/5 ÷ 8/5 = 9 ÷ 8 = 9/8. Some students might suggest that the rectangle representing each of the computations essentially "started" as the rectangle representing 9 ÷ 8, and this "original" rectangle was transformed by dividing the area, 9, and the side length, 8, by the factors 10, 4, 12, and 5, respectively. Still other students might suggest that each rectangle started as the rectangle representing 9 ÷ 8, and this rectangle was transformed by *multiplying* the area and the side lengths by the factors 1/10, 1/4, 1/12, and 1/5.

These perspectives offer an opportunity for you and the class to discuss multiplication and division as *inverse operations*. You can also point out that *reciprocal* numbers, 1/a and a (for a ≠ 0), are *multiplicative inverses* of each other, and that is why a × 1/a = 1 (see fig. 2.25).

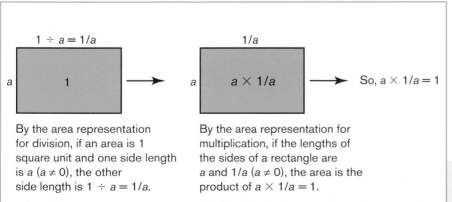

1 ÷ a = 1/a	1/a

By the area representation for division, if an area is 1 square unit and one side length is a (a ≠ 0), the other side length is 1 ÷ a = 1/a.

By the area representation for multiplication, if the lengths of the sides of a rectangle are a and 1/a (a ≠ 0), the area is the product of a × 1/a = 1.

So, a × 1/a = 1

Fig. **2.25.**

A demonstration of $a \times 1/a = 1$

The students might also suggest using the concept of direct variation to transform area representations so that the dividend and divisor are whole numbers. But if they do not, encourage them to investigate several fraction division computations by using that approach, and invite them to propose algorithms. Such algorithms might include the following steps or ideas:

1. In an area representation of division, any fraction division computation $a/b \div c/d$ (b and d not equal to zero) represents the quotient as the length of one side of a rectangle with area a/b and known side length c/d.

2. Multiplying the area and known side length first by b and then by d, or vice versa, produces an enlarged rectangle with area $a \times d$ and side lengths $b \times c$, and $a/b \div c/d = ad/bc$.

Figure 2.26 shows how one eighth-grade student, Joel, presented his argument visually.

Fig. **2.26.**

Joel's proof of $a/b \div c/d = ad/bc$

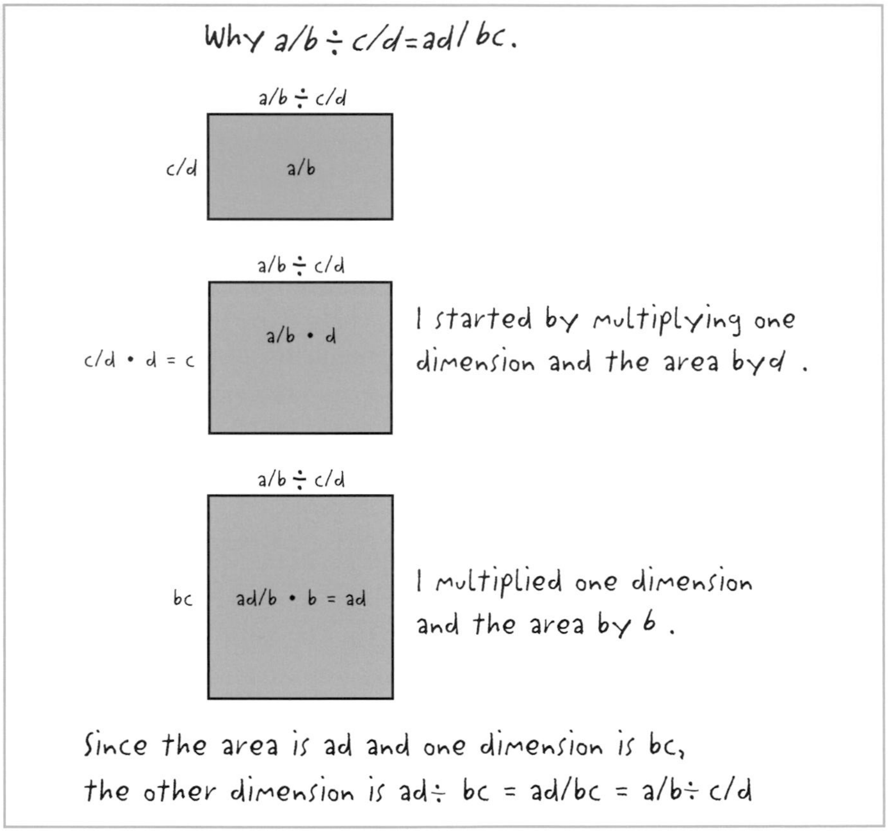

Why $a/b \div c/d = ad/bc$.

$a/b \div c/d$

c/d a/b

$a/b \div c/d$

$c/d \cdot d = c$ $a/b \cdot d$

I started by multiplying one dimension and the area by d.

$a/b \div c/d$

bc $ad/b \cdot b = ad$

I multiplied one dimension and the area by b.

Since the area is ad and one dimension is bc, the other dimension is $ad \div bc = ad/bc = a/b \div c/d$

Another approach that the students might use to test Keonna's conjecture is to determine that $9/10 \div 8/10 = 9/4 \div 8/4 = 9/12 \div 8/12 = 9/5 \div 8/5 = 9 \div 8 = 9/8$ by reasoning according to the part-to-whole representation of a fraction and the grouping representation of division. For example, one sixth-grader named David offered the following explanation; his representation appears in figure 2.27:

> Once I have equal parts, addition and subtraction of fractions are just like addition and subtraction of candy bars or apples: 9 candy bars + 8 candy bars = 17 candy bars; 9 equal pieces of candy + 8 equal pieces of candy = 17 equal pieces of candy. I just have to remember to put a denominator in my answer because

that shows the size of the pieces. It works the same for division. If I have to divide $\frac{9}{15}$ by $\frac{8}{15}$, it is just like dividing 9 pieces by 8 pieces. I have to figure out how many groups of 8 pieces are in 9 pieces. All the 15ths tell me is the size of the pieces.

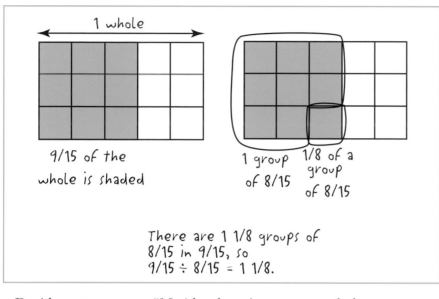

Fig. **2.27.**

David's grouping representation of 9/15 ÷ 8/15

David went on to say, "My idea doesn't seem to work the same on multiplication, though, because it seems like the size of the pieces has an effect on the answer. I'm working on that." This idea might offer a starting point for further discussion in your classroom, as might questions about the relationship of Keonna's ideas (or other ideas described here or by your students) to other operations with decimal fractions and mixed numbers.

You will have to choose which of the many worthwhile mathematical questions you want your students to investigate. The ongoing challenge of effective teaching is knowing which questions to ask, when to ask them, how to ask them so they elicit and probe students' thinking rather than suggest a certain way of thinking, when to give information, and when to let students struggle with difficult ideas.

The four activities on investigating algorithms—Linden's Algorithm, Linden's Algorithm Revisited, Erica's Algorithm, and Keonna's Conjecture—offer examples of the rich discussions that might emerge from focusing on the students' approaches for solving problems that might initially appear to be simple. By having the students also consider other students' strategies for solving the same problem, the activities help the students develop their flexibility. And by becoming more flexible, the students deepen their mathematical understanding and build fluency with operations involving rational numbers.

The next activity, Fraction Situations, provides additional opportunities for students to develop and apply new concepts that are anchored in their prior understandings. The activity encourages students to analyze the mathematical relationships in number-rich everyday situations and offers a context in which students can pose and solve problems. Thus, students have an opportunity to synthesize, apply, and enhance their understanding of concepts related to number and operations. The activity also emphasizes refining strategies through seeing, hearing, and debating other students' ideas.

Fraction Situations

Goal

* Use conceptual representations of everyday situations as the basis for posing and solving problems

Materials

For each student—

* A copy of the activity sheet "Fraction Situations"

For each pair of students—

* A half-sheet of chart paper and marking pens

For the teacher—

* An overhead projector
* Transparencies of the blackline masters "Timberline Track Team," "Jamaal's Snowstorm," and "City Soccer Fields" (available on the CD-ROM)

Activity

Distribute copies of the activity sheet "Fraction Situations," which presents three everyday scenarios with fractions in prominent roles. The students must make diagrams that show the mathematical relationships, compose questions that their diagrams can help them consider, and answer their questions, explaining their reasoning. Begin by placing a transparency of the blackline master "Timberline Track Team" (situation 1; see facing page) on the overhead projector. Allow the students several minutes to work individually to generate ideas about the situation. Then arrange the students in pairs and have them discuss their ideas and adapt, refine, and extend their questions and visual solutions. Give each pair of students a half-sheet of chart paper and ask them to record the diagrams, questions, solutions, and reasoning on which they have reached a consensus. Encourage the students to note aspects of the situations or their questions that stumped them as well as parts of the problem-solving process that made them think, "Aha." Also ask the students to record the computations that correspond to their visual models whenever possible.

After the student pairs have completed the task, ask each pair to team with another pair to share their work. Observe the interactions, and collect ideas that the whole class should discuss. Next, facilitate a large-group discussion of the "big ideas" that the students observed as well as any "burning questions" that they raised. Post the students' diagrams and solutions around the classroom so that the students will have an opportunity to observe and think about other strategies. Repeat this process for the other two situations in the activity.

Discussion

When students confront scenarios that do not pose questions, they focus on relationships rather than on "getting answers." Asking their own questions increases motivation and heightens access for all students.

You can also base important assessments on the questions that students pose, the concepts and strategies that they use in their solutions, and their persistence in asking more complex questions or generalizing about the situations. Such experiences give students opportunities to synthesize, apply, and enhance their understanding of number and operations.

The following examples show the representations, questions, and solution strategies devised by middle school students for the three situations in this activity. These examples illustrate ways in which students might think about and approach these situations. Many other approaches exist. Be sure to encourage your students to think through the situations in ways that make sense to them. Allow time for the students to see, hear, and debate the different ideas and approaches of other students (including the ideas in these examples). This process will enable all your students to broaden and refine their strategies.

These examples of students' work illustrate what some students *might* do—not what they *should* do.

Allow your students to think through their own solutions. Then give them the opportunity to see, hear, and debate a range of other students' ideas and approaches.

Through this process, the students can both broaden and refine their own strategies and mathematical thinking.

Fraction Situation 1—Timberline Track Team

At Timberline Middle School, $\frac{5}{8}$ of the sixth-grade class are girls, and $\frac{2}{3}$ of the sixth-grade girls are on the track team. All the sixth-grade boys are on the track team.

Mario and Paulina worked together on this situation. They represented their work as shown in figure 2.28.

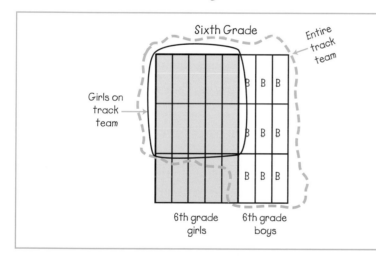

Fig. **2.28.**

Mario and Paulina's work on "Timberline Track Team"

Mario and Paulina's reasoning about the scenario follows:

First we drew a square that represents the whole class. Then we divided the square into 8 columns and shaded 5 of the columns to stand for the girls in the sixth grade. Next, we divided the square into 3 rows. We put Bs in the parts that stand for the boys. We looped $\frac{2}{3}$ of the girls to show the girls on the track team. We drew a cloud around the boys and girls on the track team. Once we got the sketch into equal parts, we could answer all these questions just by looking at our diagram:

• What fraction of the sixth grade are boys?

$\frac{9}{24}$

- What fraction of the total students are on the track team?
  $\frac{9}{24} + \frac{10}{24} = \frac{19}{24}$

- What fraction of the students are not on the track team?
  $\frac{5}{24} = \frac{24}{24} - \frac{19}{24}$

- Are there more boys or girls on the track team?
  Girls, because $\frac{10}{19}$ of the team are girls and $\frac{9}{19}$ are boys.

- What is the ratio of the number of girls on the track team to the number of girls not on the track team?
  2 to 1

- The number of boys on the team is how many times the number of girls on the team?
  Even though we don't know the number of girls or boys, we can see $\frac{9}{19}$ as many boys as girls in our diagram.

- The number of girls on the team is how many times the number of boys on the team?
  We determined that $1\frac{1}{9}$ group of boys (9 parts) makes the group of girls (10 parts). Another way to say this is $1\frac{1}{9} \times \frac{9}{24} = \frac{10}{24}$, and even another way to say it is $\frac{10}{24} \div \frac{9}{24} = 1\frac{1}{9}$. But we didn't use algorithms to solve those, we just looked at our diagram and could see the answers.

Other questions that your students might ask or that you could pose to those who have run out of ideas include the following:

- "What numbers of students (girls and boys) could be in the sixth grade?"

- "What computations could you write to represent what you see in the diagrams?"

- "What if $\frac{1}{5}$ of the girls on the track team decided to drop out?"

Fraction Situation 2—Jamaal's Snowstorm

After a heavy January snowstorm, the snow in Jamaal's front yard was 42 inches deep, which is $3\frac{1}{2}$ times as deep as it was before the storm. The amount of new snow that fell during the storm is $\frac{5}{6}$ of the all-time record for a snowstorm in Jamaal's state.

Rumiana and Jewel worked together on this scenario. Figure 2.29 shows their initial diagram.

Fig. **2.29.**

Rumiana and Jewel's work on "Jamaal's Snowstorm"

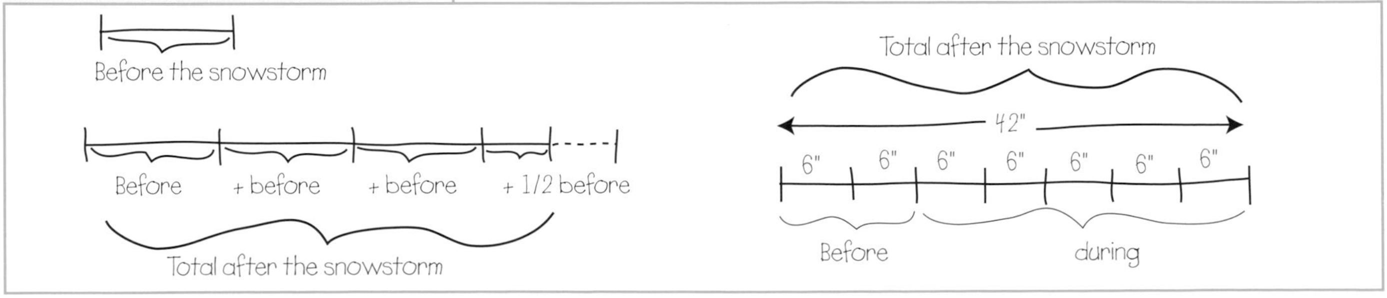

Rumiana and Jewel described their approach as follows, and figure 2.30 shows how they represented the last step.

First, we drew a length to stand for how deep the snow was before the storm. Then we connected $3\frac{1}{2}$ copies of that length to stand for how deep the snow was after the storm. We noticed that we could divide each of the 3 copies into 2 equal parts. When we combined those with the $\frac{1}{2}$ copy, we had 7 equal parts and each part is 42 inches ÷ 7 = 6 inches long.

Here are questions we can answer about the situation:
- How deep was the snow before and after the storm?
  12 inches (before) and 42 inches (after)
- How much snow fell during the storm?
  42 inches – 12 inches = 30 inches
- How much is $42 \div 3\frac{1}{2}$?
  12, that's how much is in each whole group after we split 42 into $3\frac{1}{2}$ equal groups.
- How much was the record snowfall?
  36 inches. We used a drawing to figure it out.

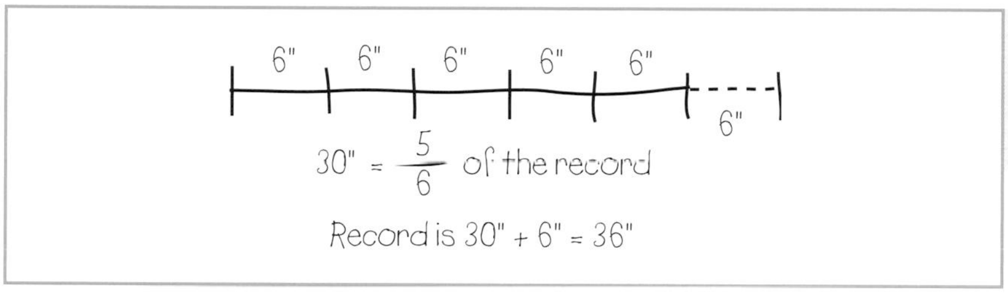

Fig. **2.30.**

Rumiana and Jewel's diagram for finding the depth of the record snowfall

Fraction Situation 3—City Soccer Fields

The city parks department purchased land for new soccer fields. This rectangular plot of land covers $\frac{3}{4}$ of a square mile and is bordered on one side by a road that is $\frac{2}{3}$ of a mile long. Fencing costs $4400 per $\frac{1}{4}$ of a mile. Grass seed costs $40 per 25-pound bag. Five pounds of grass seed cover $\frac{1}{5}$ of a square mile.

Ramon and Carla started thinking about this situation by using an area representation of division in which the area of a rectangle and the length of one dimension are given. Figure 2.31 shows their representation of their work, and their description of their reasoning follows:

First we drew a rectangle with an area of $\frac{3}{4}$ square mile and side length of $\frac{2}{3}$ mile. We decided that we wanted to know the length of the other side, which is the answer to $\frac{3}{4} \div \frac{2}{3}$. Our diagram shows how we figured out the other side length.

These are our questions and answers:
- How long is the other side of the property?
  $1\frac{1}{8}$ miles

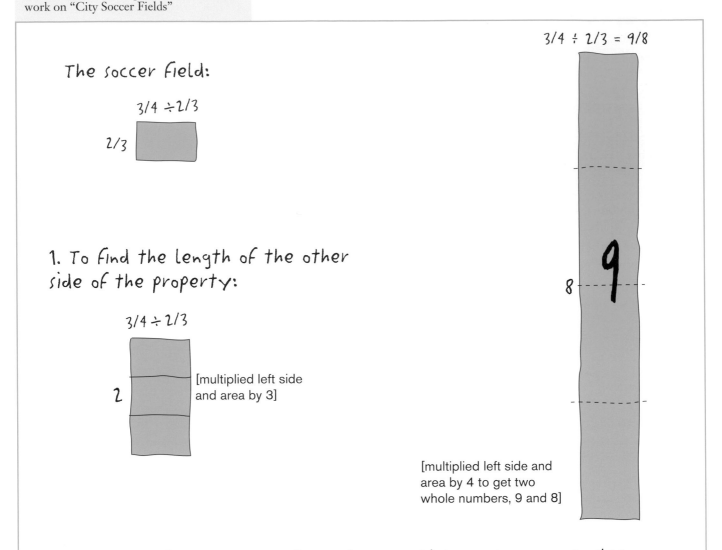

The soccer field:

$3/4 \div 2/3$

$2/3$

**1. To find the length of the other
side of the property:**

$3/4 \div 2/3$

2

[multiplied left side
and area by 3]

$3/4 \div 2/3 = 9/8$

9

8

[multiplied left side and
area by 4 to get two
whole numbers, 9 and 8]

**2. To determine the cost of the fence, which we know costs $4400 per
quarter mile, or $17,600 per mile:**

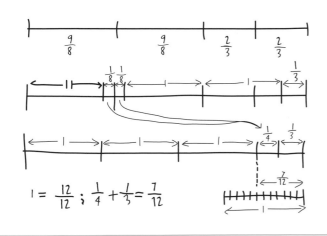

Perimeter = 1 + 1 + 1 + 1/4 + 1/3

= 3 + 7/12 = 3 7/12 miles

Cost of fence

= 3 × $17,600 + cost of 7/12 mile

= $52,800 + cost of 2 1/3 quarter miles

= $52,800 + $4400 + $4400 + $1467 (rounded)

≈ $63,067

- What is the perimeter of the property?

  $3\frac{7}{12}$ miles. Here is how we thought about it:

  $\frac{2}{3} + \frac{2}{3} + 1\frac{1}{8} + 1\frac{1}{8} = \frac{4}{3} + 2\frac{1}{4} = 1\frac{1}{3} + 2\frac{1}{4} = 3 + \frac{1}{3} + \frac{1}{4}$.

  We remembered from our work with egg cartons that

  $\frac{1}{3} + \frac{1}{4} = \frac{4}{12} + \frac{3}{12}$, so the answer is $3 + \frac{4}{12} + \frac{3}{12} = 3\frac{7}{12}$ miles.

- How much will the fence cost if they fence the whole property?

  $63,067. Since the fence costs $4400 for every quarter mile, we multiplied $4400 by 4 to figure how much one mile costs. That's $17,600. So $3\frac{7}{12}$ miles costs $3 \times \$17,600$ + the cost of $\frac{7}{12}$ mile. Next, we figured how many $\frac{1}{4}$ are in $\frac{7}{12}$ (that's $\frac{7}{12} \div \frac{1}{4}$, but we solved it visually). That's $2\frac{1}{3}$, so we know the $\frac{7}{12}$ mile of fence will cost $4400 + $4400 + $\frac{1}{3}$ of $4400. Altogether the cost of the fence equals $52,800 + $4400 + $4400 + $1467 (rounded) = $63,067.

- How much will grass seed cost if they plant grass on all the property?

  $40, because they need to buy one bag, but they will only use $30 worth of the seed. That is because 5 pounds of grass seed covers $\frac{1}{5}$ square mile, so a 25-pound bag covers 1 square mile. Since the area of the property is $\frac{3}{4}$ square mile, they only need $\frac{3}{4}$ of a bag. Since one bag costs $40, then $\frac{3}{4}$ of a bag is worth $30.

You or your students might also ask, "What if 5 pounds of grass seed covered $\frac{2}{5}$ square mile? $\frac{2}{3}$ square mile?"

You might work with your students to develop a scoring guide for assessing their work on situations such as these. The students could use the scoring guide to assess their own or one another's work.

Many problem-solving resources (even some old textbooks) offer engaging situations that you can use like the scenarios in this activity. Just remove the questions before you present them to students.

Extensions

It may be helpful to review some concepts in this chapter and high-light resources on the CD-ROM that can help you and your students explore these ideas further.

Developing Flexibility and the Ability to Generalize

The activities in chapter 2 can help you foster your students' *flexibility* and *ability to generalize*. These two skills can help the students come to a richer understanding of the meanings of addition, subtraction, multiplication, and division as they extend the use of these operations from whole numbers to rational numbers. The series of activities on investigating algorithms (Linden's Algorithm, Linden's Algorithm Revisited, Erica's Algorithm, and Keonna's Conjecture) provide examples of the rich discussions that can develop as students work to solve what might appear to be a simple problem—for example, to illustrate the meaning(s) of 2/3 × 4/5 and demonstrate a visual strategy for determining the product. The activities encourage students to (a) create visual representations for a problem, (b) use these representations to help them solve the problem, (c) understand and apply the visual strategies of other students, and (d) ultimately move from applying these visual solutions to creating generalizations and algorithms for working with rational numbers.

The *ability to generalize* refers not only to students' skill in making generalizations but also to their capacity to recognize that a particular situation fits the conditions of a known generalization. For students to develop an ability to generalize, it is not enough that they see and apply generalizations—they must also learn to make and test their own generalizations (Rachlin 1998; available on the CD-ROM). The activity Fraction Situations offers different contexts for students to pose and solve problems and provides opportunities for them to synthesize, apply, and enhance their understanding of operations with rational numbers. Giving students a chance to see, hear, and debate a range of other students' ideas and approaches allows them to enrich their own strategies.

You can evaluate your students' progress toward developing these abilities through activities like the ones in this chapter. Even changing the way that a problem is posed can yield insight about students' abilities while simultaneously strengthening them. For example, Rachlin (1998) shows that simply changing the problem, "Multiply 2/3 × 9/4," to, "What number multiplied by 2/3 equals 3/2?" changed the ways that a group of students thought about the multiplication of fractions. Many students simply multiplied 2/3 × 3/2; others were unsure whether to represent the problem as 3/2 ÷ 2/3, or 2/3 ÷ 3/2. Often, students are rule-oriented, and they tend to state generalizations about the solution process before beginning the problem. In many instances, they over-generalize something that occurs in the problem or something that the teacher said. Rachlin (1998) identified the following ways in which the students correctly solved the problem:

- Kathy solved the problem like an equation. First, she wrote $\frac{2}{3}n = \frac{3}{2}$, then she multiplied both sides of the equation by $\frac{3}{2}$.
- Curtis said that he found common denominators for the $\frac{2}{3}$ and $\frac{3}{2}$ and then rewrote the problem $\frac{4}{6} \times ? = \frac{9}{6}$. But $6 \times 1 = 6$ and $4 \times \frac{9}{4} = 9$, so the answer was $\frac{\frac{9}{4}}{1}$.
- Margaret multiplied the $\frac{2}{3}$ by $\frac{3}{2}$ to get 1. Then she multiplied the 1 by $\frac{3}{2}$ to get $\frac{3}{2}$. She wrote this as $(\frac{2}{3} \times \frac{3}{2}) \times \frac{3}{2} = \frac{3}{2}$. The fraction she was looking for was $(\frac{3}{2} \times \frac{3}{2})$ or $\frac{9}{4}$.
- Lani wrote the $\frac{3}{2}$ as an equivalent fraction such that 2 would divide into its numerator evenly and 3 would divide into its denominator evenly. She chose $\frac{18}{12}$ as a fraction equivalent to $\frac{3}{2}$ that met these conditions. Then $\frac{2}{3} \times ? = \frac{18}{12}$. Since $18 \div 2 = 9$ and $12 \div 3 = 4$, she decided her solution was $\frac{9}{4}$.

In "Learning to See the Wind," Rachlin (1998; available on the CD-ROM) says, "Flexibility is the ability to switch from thinking of one method of solving a problem to another. How a student perceives a problem shapes the processes that she or he may bring to bear on the solution of the problem. The various solution paths that a student selects establish the structure for the problem." (p. 471)

- Joe wrote $\frac{2}{3} \times (\ \ ) = \frac{3}{2}$ and then he filled in the parentheses. Since he wanted to get a 2 in the denominator, he needed a 2 in the denominator of the fraction in parentheses. But that 2 would "cancel" with the 2 in the numerator of the $\frac{2}{3}$, so he needed a 4 in the denominator of the fraction in the parentheses. Similarly, he said that he needed a 9 in the numerator. (p. 472)

Taken collectively, methods such as these help give students a more robust conceptual understanding of the multiplication of fractions.

Additional Resources on Students' Conceptual Understanding of Operations with Rational Numbers

The activities in chapter 2 are designed to extend students' conceptual understanding of the algorithms for addition, subtraction, multiplication, and division to include fractions as well as whole numbers. The CD-ROM accompanying this book includes resources to help you broaden this development.

Algorithms with Decimals. Chappell and Thompson (1999; available on the CD-ROM) discuss building reversibility, flexibility, and an ability to generalize by changing routine questions into tasks that support the development of students' conceptual understanding of decimals— including their senses of number, number relationships, operations, and applications. Such approaches can help students extend what they have learned about fractions to decimals. Here are some samples of tasks that Chappell and Thompson (1999) created to reveal students' mathematical understanding:

- Reversibility
  a. Make up a word problem whose answer is given by 5.68 × 2.34.
  b. Juanita divided 70 by a mystery number and got 2.63 for an answer. Is the mystery number bigger or smaller than 70? How do you know?

- Ability to Generalize
  a. Without dividing, estimate which of the following has the smallest quotient:
    4.9 ÷ 0.003, 4.9 ÷ 0.03, 4.9 ÷ 0.3, 4.9 ÷ 3.
  b. Do 0.3 and 0.30 name the same amount? Explain your answer.

- Flexibility
    Name a decimal that estimates the value of point *A*.

  Why did you give *A* that value? (p. 471)

Facility and Fluency with Rational Numbers. Developing a conceptual understanding of operations with rational numbers is necessary for

See "Developing Algorithms for Adding and Subtracting Fractions" (Lappan and Bouck 1998) on the CD-ROM.

applying such operations in nonroutine situations. However, having a conceptual understanding supports but does not guarantee facility and fluency with the operations. Students enhance these skills as they develop the ability to assess the reasonableness of a solution for a particular problem and improve their efficiency and accuracy in applying appropriate algorithms.

The CD-ROM also features activities designed to develop students' facility and fluency in working with rational numbers. Lappan and Bouck (1998; available on the CD-ROM) show how middle school curricular materials that encourage students to develop algorithms for adding and subtracting fractions help students develop their understanding, ability to add and subtract fractions, and ability to assess the reasonableness of a solution for a given problem. The authors point out that students' invented algorithms are often very efficient—and often resemble standard algorithms. With a teacher's help, the authors say, such algorithms can become powerful and generalizable. Lappan and Bouck present a series of problems to guide students in creating algorithms. They explain students' solution strategies and show how, through such experiences, students gain understanding of the meanings of the operations.

Students gain facility with operations involving rational numbers as they gain a greater sense of the reasonableness of their answers. Reys (1986) offers tools for helping students with concepts of reasonableness. Reys describes strategies that teachers can encourage students to use for estimating and determining the reasonableness of answers, including answers to problems with fractions, decimals, and percents.

The applet Adding Decimals—Circle 3 on the CD-ROM engages students in an interactive game that promotes their fluency and accuracy in adding decimals.

One distinction between activities designed to help students understand operations with rational numbers and activities designed to help students gain fluency and facility with these operations is that activities of the second type encourage efficiency and accuracy. The applet Adding Decimals—Circle 3 offers an interactive activity that allows the students to practice adding decimals. Figure 2.32 presents a sample Circle 3 problem. Students position decimal numbers inside the circles and their intersections in such a way that the three decimal numbers in each of the circles add to 3. Students drag and drop numbers to positions in the ring of circles. When the three numbers in a circle add up to 3, the circle changes color. Rather than offer a page of addition problems, Adding Decimals—Circle 3 provides a problem-solving setting in which students perform a series of problems involving the addition of decimals. The task encourages efficiency and accuracy.

Conclusion

Chapter 2 has emphasized building students' conceptual understanding of operations with rational numbers. Chapter 3 discusses ways of significantly extending students' understanding of important ideas of the rational numbers and their operations. It features mathematical activities that promote developing an understanding of proportionality through problem solving and reasoning.

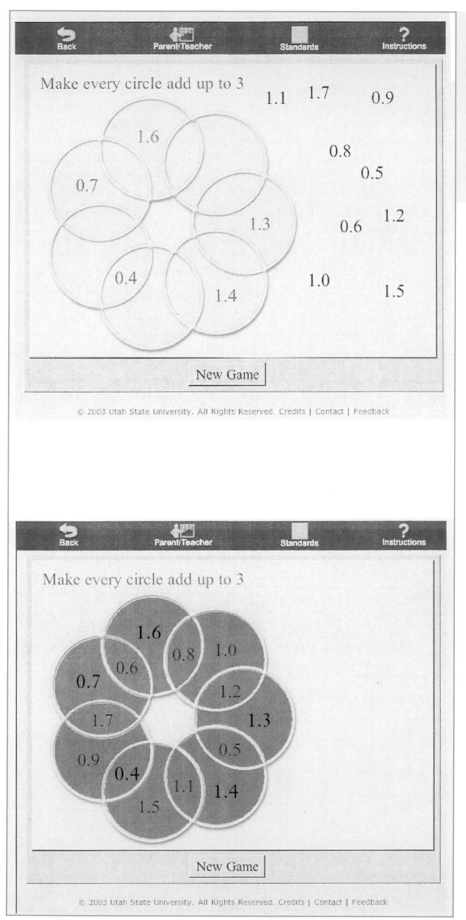

Fig. **2.32.**

A sample from the applet Adding Decimals—Circle 3 (applet created by and used with permission of Utah State University; figure does not show applet's actual colors). Students are given the circles and must place the remaining numbers on the game board to make every circle add up to 3. The top screen shows the problem, and the bottom screen shows the solution.

NAVIGATIONS SERIES

GRADES 6–8

NAVIGATING *through* NUMBER *and* OPERATIONS

Chapter 3
Proportional Reasoning

Important Mathematical Ideas

Principles and Standards for School Mathematics (NCTM 2000) identifies proportionality as an integrative theme in middle school mathematics programs. Students can develop facility with proportionality by exploring many real-world phenomena. Proportions are involved in such tasks as using a map scale to determine the actual distance between two cities, comparing two runners' rates of speed to determine who is running faster, and working with unit prices to determine which brand of frozen pizza is a better buy. Likewise, within the study of mathematics, many concepts encountered in the middle grades involve proportions, including similarity, the relationship between the circumference and diameter of a circle, and probability. Students can approach such topics by using proportionality as a framework for understanding.

Identifying Multiplicative Relationships

Being able to solve problems that reflect proportional situations involves more than solving traditional missing-value problems by using the standard cross-product algorithm. Beneath all proportional contexts lies a multiplicative relationship between the quantities that represent the situation. This multiplicative relationship can and should be viewed in multiple representations, like patterns in data tables, graphs, and equations. By comparing proportional contexts with nonproportional contexts, students can strengthen their understanding of the multiplicative relationship behind proportions.

"Instruction in solving proportions should include methods that have a strong intuitive basis."
(NCTM 2000, p. 221)

Figure 3.1 shows such contexts involving the rates of two taxicab companies. For each company, the students must find the cost of a 12-mile ride. The table helps represent the numerical relationships between the quantities *distance* and *cost*. For each company, the students know the same details—the fee, the distance, and that the number of miles in a ride is calculated by adding an additional mile for any fractional part of a mile. For example, a ride of 2.25 miles is treated as if it were 3 miles. The tables show similar growth in cost as the distance increases. In the table for the Harmony Taxicab Company, the cost increases by a constant amount of $3 as the number of miles increases by one mile. The cost of a ride with the Eureka Taxicab Company increases by a constant amount of $2 as the number of miles increases by one mile. This constant growth in each table shows that a linear relationship exists between miles and cost for each company. The linear relationships between the two quantities, miles and cost, can be modeled algebraically in two ways for each company. With d as the distance expressed as a whole number of miles, and c as the cost in dollars, the Harmony Taxicab Company's rate can be represented as $c = 3d$, or $d = (1/3)c$. The Eureka Taxicab Company's rate can be represented as $c = 2d + 1.5$, or $d = (c - 1.5)/2$.

Fig. **3.1.**

Proportional and nonproportional situations involving the rates of two taxicab companies

Thompson and Bush (2003; available on the CD-ROM) note,

"For middle school teachers to help their students become proportional reasoners, they must understand the characteristics of proportional reasoning and know that it is developmental, emerges gradually, and grows over a span of several years. Teaching students to solve proportions by using the cross-product method alone does not develop the students' proportional reasoning skills. Proportional reasoning is a way of thinking, not an algorithm to be used in solving problems." (p. 400)

Proportional

The Harmony Taxicab Company in Harmony, Arkansas, charges $3.00 per mile (rounded up to the next mile). How much would a 12-mile ride cost?

Distance in miles	1	2	3	4	5	6
Cost in dollars	$3.00	$6.00	$9.00	$12.00	$15.00	$18.00

Nonproportional

The Eureka Taxicab Company in Eureka Springs, Arkansas, charges a basic fee of $1.50, plus $2.00 per mile (rounded up to the next mile). How much would a 12-mile ride cost?

Distance in miles	1	2	3	4	5	6
Cost in dollars	$3.50	$5.50	$7.50	$9.50	$11.50	$13.50

Comparing the two functions enables students to see that the essential feature of a proportional situation is the multiplicative relationship between the two quantities. For Harmony Taxicab's rates, multiplication completely defines the relationship between miles and cost, making it proportional. The cost of any whole number of miles can be found by multiplying the number of miles by $3; the distance, rounded up to the next mile, can be found by multiplying the cost by 1/3 or dividing by 3.

These *constant factors* also describe the cost per mile ($3 per 1 mile) or distance per dollar (1/3 mile per dollar). Both these relationships are *unit rates*. By contrast, for Eureka Taxicab, addition or subtraction of the base fee of $1.50 partly defines the relationship between miles and cost; therefore, the relationship is not proportional. The cost for the actual distance is found by multiplying the number of miles (rounded up to the next mile) by $2 and adding $1.50; the distance is found by subtracting $1.50 from the total cost and then dividing by 2 or multiplying by 1/2. The situation involves no constant unit rates.

In a proportional situation, because multiplication defines the relationship between the two quantities (in this case, miles and cost), other multiplicative relationships exist and can be seen in tables representing the situations. For example, in the table for Harmony Taxicab, multiplying each of the values in column 3—2 miles and $6—by 3 gives another rate pair in the table: 6 miles for $18. Students might express this relationship by saying, "If I triple the number of miles, the cost will also triple." Thus, to determine the cost of a 12-mile ride, a student could double 6 miles and $18. This type of multiplicative relationship is characteristic of proportional situations and is often referred to as a *scale factor*. No such multiplicative relationship exists in nonproportional situations. Doubling (or tripling) any number of miles in the table for Eureka Taxicab does not result in a doubling (or tripling) of the corresponding number of dollars.

Gerard Vergnaud (1983) uses the term *measure space* in his description of the multiplicative relationships existing in proportional situations. The idea of measure spaces might help clarify for students the different multiplicative relationships inherent in proportional situations. In the table in the margin, "bags" and "cost" are two measure spaces. In proportional situations, a constant multiplicative relationship exists *across* measure spaces. Here, the relationship is *cost = 3 × number of bags*. Because the constant is an integer, the proportional situation can be described as having an *integer relationship*. A constant multiplicative relationship also exists *within* measure spaces. Increasing the number of bags by a certain factor results in the corresponding cost increasing by that same factor. Here, 2 bags increased by a factor of 2.5 corresponds to a cost that is 2.5 times $6.00, or $15.00. This *within* multiplicative relationship is often called the *scale factor*.

Having students record data in a table as a set of rates can help them observe another characteristic of proportional situations. The cost/miles rates for Harmony Taxicab would be 3/1, 6/2, 9/3, and 12/4. These rates are all equivalent to 3/1, the constant factor relating miles and cost as seen in the rule $c = 3d$. The rate 3/1 is the *unit rate*, or cost per mile. A different set of equivalent rates can be generated by considering the reciprocal rates, miles/cost. These rates, 1/3, 2/6, 3/9, and so forth, are all equal to 1/3, the constant factor in the second possible function rule for the data, $d = (1/3)c$. Furthermore, 1/3 can be interpreted as a *unit rate*, 1/3 of a mile per dollar. Equivalent rates do not occur for the nonproportional Eureka Taxicab situation—3.50/1, 5.50/2, 7.50/3 are not equivalent rates, and neither are their reciprocals.

Representing data on a coordinate axis can highlight the multiplicative relationship inherent in proportional situations in yet another way. Figure 3.2 shows graphs of both taxicab functions with the independent

Bags	Cost
2	$6.00
5	$15.00

Fig. **3.2.**

Graphs of the taxicab companies' rates

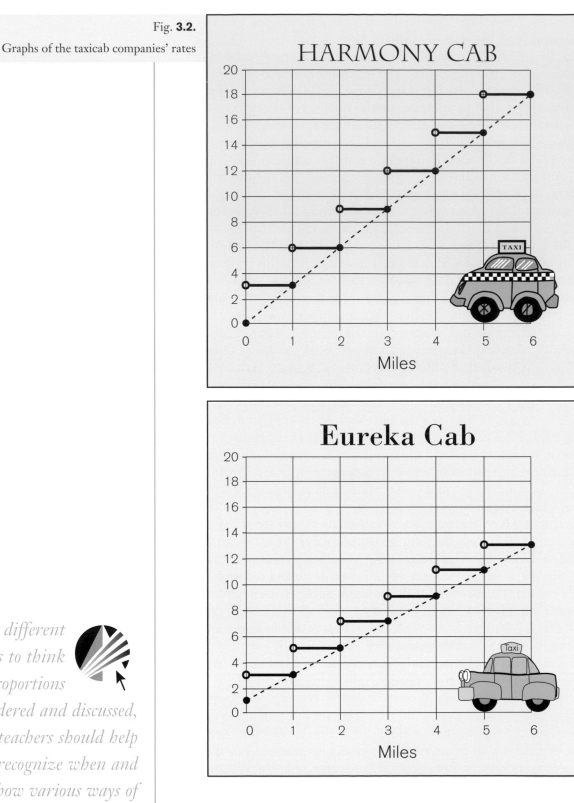

variable as miles. The solid line segments reflect the fact that miles in this scenario must be rounded up to the next mile. For example, the actual charge for traveling $1\frac{1}{3}$ miles is $6 with Harmony Taxicab. The dotted lines represent the underlying mathematics of the functions for all real numbers—that is, with no rounding up. Although both functions for the dotted lines are linear with positive slopes, the graph of the proportional Harmony Taxicab rates intersects the origin, but the graph of Eureka Taxicab rates does not. The dotted line for $c = 3d$ intersects the origin because multiplication exclusively defines the underlying relationship between miles and cost. The nonproportional Eureka Taxicab context is defined by both multiplication and addition, with addition represented in the graph by the dotted line crossing the y-axis at 1.5. The slope of the dotted line for the proportional Harmony Taxicab situation is 3, which is the constant factor relating miles and cost in the function $c = 3d$, as well as the unit rate of cost per mile.

As students begin to explore proportional situations, they should learn to recognize these characteristics:

- A constant multiplicative relationship exists between two quantities and can be expressed algebraically in two ways.

- All rates describing a given proportional situation are equivalent, as are the reciprocals of these rates. In the Harmony Taxicab example, the rates are $3/1 mile or 1/3 mile per one dollar. In these forms, the rates are unit rates.

- The rate and its reciprocal are the constants of proportionality and define the multiplicative relationship between quantities.

- The rule defining the multiplicative relationship is always in the form $y = mx$, with m as one of the constants of proportionality. In the Harmony Taxicab example, the two possible rules are $c = 3d$ and $d = (1/3)c$.

- Graphically, all points fall on a straight line passing through the origin. In real-world situations, these lines have positive slopes.

- The slope of the line, m, which is one of the constants of proportionality relating the two quantities, corresponds to one of the unit rates.

Types of Proportional Reasoning Problems

Solving different types of problems embedded in real-world contexts helps students in the middle grades develop their proportional reasoning skills. Researchers have used a variety of tasks to explore students' proportional reasoning. These tasks offer frameworks from which you can develop creative problems for classroom instruction and assessment (Cramer, Post, and Currier 1993; Heller et al. 1990; Karplus, Pulos, and Stage 1983). Figure 3.3 shows four types of proportional reasoning problems from different research projects. Before students learn standard procedures for solving proportional reasoning tasks, they should have the opportunity to solve problems like these four types by constructing their own solution strategies.

Missing-value problems represent the most common type of proportional reasoning tasks in traditional curricula. One example is the Tall Man–Short Man task designed by Karplus, Pulos, and Stage (1983) to investigate students' solution strategies in a missing-value situation. Students are given a picture labeled "Mr. Short," a chain of paper clips, and information that Mr. Short's height is 4 buttons. Students then measure Mr. Short and find that his height is 6 paper clips. Next, students are told that Mr. Tall, a figure they cannot see, is 6 buttons tall. They must then determine Mr. Tall's height in paper clips.

Cramer, Post, and Currier (1993) provide a synthesis of the research on proportional reasoning and an anaylsis of its implications for the middle school classroom.

Problem Type	Familiar Context	Less Familiar Context
Missing value	You are buying some candy for the end-of-the-year party. Green's Corner Store is selling 2 bags for $6. You want to buy 10 bags for the class party. How much will they cost? Explain your reasoning.	The scale on a map shows that 3 cm equals 25 km. If the map distance is 20 cm, what is the actual distance? Explain your reasoning.
Numerical comparison	William runs around the track every day after school. Today he ran 3 laps in 9 minutes. Yesterday he ran 7 laps in 21 minutes. On which day did he run faster, or did he run at the same pace on both days? Explain your reasoning.	The Bank of Honolulu offers an exchange rate of £2 for $3. The London Bank offers a rate of £5 for $9. Compare the two rates.
Qualitative comparison	If William mixed less flavor-aid powder with more water than Annie did, whose flavor-aid mixture is stronger, or are they the same? Explain your reasoning.	If there are more people living in an area in Newark than in an area of the same size in Greenwich, in which city do you suppose that the people live closer together, or does the density seem to be the same?
Qualitative prediction	Mark rides his bike every day. If he takes longer today to travel the same distance that he traveled yesterday, did his speed increase, decrease, stay the same, or can't you tell? Explain your reasoning.	If the London Bank exchanges more pounds for fewer U.S. dollars today than it did yesterday, then would today's exchange rate, £ to $, be greater than, less than, or the same as yesterday's rate, or can't you tell? Explain your reasoning.

Numerical comparison tasks are similar to fraction-order tasks, but they are embedded in a real-world context. One example is the orange juice task (Noelting 1980), which has been used to research students' proportional reasoning strategies on numerical comparison tasks. In this problem, students determine the relative strengths of two orange juice mixtures from the number of glasses of orange juice concentrate and the number of glasses of water for the two mixtures. Students first have to imagine mixing the orange juice concentrate and water in a container, and then they have to determine which mixture has the stronger orange taste.

Research shows that students' strategies in missing-value and numerical comparison tasks are often affected by the context and the complexity of the numbers. Students have more success in solving problems embedded in familiar contexts than in solving problems involving less familiar situations. Numerical characteristics have even more impact on students' success with proportional reasoning tasks, influencing both the type of strategy that the students use and their level of success in solving the problem (Karplus, Pulos, and Stage 1983). The easiest proportional reasoning problems are embedded in familiar situations involving numbers with integer relationships (that is, where the constant multiplicative relationships *across* and *within* measure spaces are integers).

Strive to help your students develop a flexible repertoire of strategies and an understanding of the connections among them. At some point in their middle-grades years, students' thinking should become sufficiently stable that context and "awkward" numbers no longer affect their ability to solve proportional reasoning problems.

Important nontraditional tasks that students should experience include *qualitative comparison* and *qualitative prediction*. Such problems do not provide specific numbers; therefore, students cannot use rote numerical rules to solve them. These problems instead require the students to think about the quantities involved and how they are related. Their analyses might involve inferring the effect of changing a rate's numerator or its denominator on the rate. Experiences with such problems will also support students' solutions to numerical problems. When they think qualitatively, students can establish reasonable parameters for solving numerical problems and can check the feasibility of their answers.

As you try to foster your students' proportional reasoning skills in grades 6–8, expose them to a variety of problem types. The strategies that they learn will bolster their understanding of proportionality and of broader concepts within the area of number and operations. The activity Changing Rates, which appears later in this chapter, will give your students experiences with qualitative prediction.

Developing Unit-Rate Strategies

One proportional reasoning strategy that students often employ on their own is a unit-rate strategy. Even without formal instruction, a number of your students are likely to find and use unit rates to solve missing-value and numerical comparison problems. Presenting such problems to your students and taking opportunities to discuss any unit-rate strategies that they use can help you reinforce their skills in proportional reasoning.

You will probably notice that the context and the presence of integer relationships between quantities influence students' use of unit-rate strategies. Consider the experiences of one sixth-grade class in solving two missing-value and numerical comparison problems. In the first problem, a missing-value task, the students had to determine the cost of 5 bags of candy when two bags cost $6. Figure 3.4 shows the following ways that the unit rate, cost per bag, appeared in students' solutions: (a) students found the cost per bag and multiplied that by the number of bags; (b) students found the cost for one bag and generated the cost for 2, 3, 4, and then 5 bags; and (c) students found the cost for

Billings (2001; available on the CD-ROM), defines *proportion sense* as "the ability to reason about quantities and the various relationships that quantities share in proportional situations" (p. 11), and offers a variety of examples supporting the use of nonnumeric problems to encourage the development of students' proportion sense.

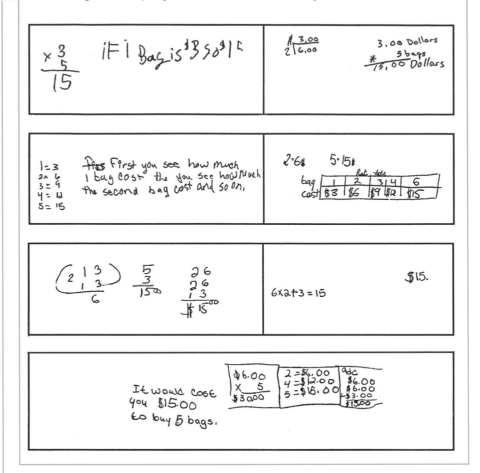

1. You are buying candy for a class party. The local supermarket is selling two bags of chocolate bars for $6. You want to buy five bags for the party. How much will this cost you?

4 bags and then added the cost for one bag. The fact that students encounter unit pricing outside the mathematics classroom might explain why ten out of eighteen students in the class used unit rates.

The second problem called for a numerical comparison, asking the students to compare the price of two bags of chocolate bars at the supermarket to the price of two bags of the same candy at the drugstore to determine which store was offering the better buy. (See fig. 3.5.) Although the strategy of comparing rates by reflecting on the numerator (the first strategy in fig. 3.5) might appear to be the most obvious way to compare the two rates, only a few students used that strategy. Instead, a significant number of students focused on the cost for one bag of candy, and that calculation played a role in most of the correct solutions from this particular class. The students either found the unit rate for both stores and compared the cost for one bag or used the unit rate to find and compare the total costs for buying the same quantity from both stores.

That students often construct a unit rate to solve proportional problems should not be surprising, because the familiar one-step multiplication and division problems introduced in third grade are unit-rate problems. Consider the following two problems:

2. At the drugstore you see that you can buy two bags of the same chocolate bars as in problem 1 [see fig. 3.4] for $5. Which offers the better buy, the supermarket or the drugstore?

Fig. **3.5.**

Sixth-grade students' solutions to a numerical-comparison problem in a buying context

Comparing rates by reflecting on the numerator

The better buy would be at the drugstore because you can buy two bags at the drugstore for five dollars and if you bought two bags at the supermarket it would be six dollars

Comparing cost per bag

the drugstore is a better buy. It cost $.50 less a bag.

The Drugstore is better because one bag is for 2.50 and the supermarket is $.50 more. than at the drugstore

Comparing total costs

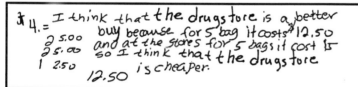

$ 4. =
2)5.00
2)5.00
1 2.50
    12.50

I think that the drugstore is a better buy because for 5 bag it costs $12.50 and at the stores for 5 bags it cost $ so I think that the drugstore is cheaper.

$ 12.50

4 = $10
1 = 2.50

the drugstore is better buy, it costs less money.

the drugstore is the better buy you save $2.50

$2.50
2)5.00
 4
 0

2.50
2.50
3.00

2.50
  5
12.50

1. If two bags of candy cost $6, how much does one bag of candy cost?

2. If candy costs $3 per bag, how much will 5 bags cost?

Solving the first problem involves dividing to find the unit rate: $6 per 2 bags = $3 per bag. Solving the second problem involves multiplying the given unit rate, $3/bag, by 5 bags to find the total cost. The missing-value problem in figure 3.4 simply extends these one-step multiplication and division problems. To find the missing value, many students first find the unit rate and use the rate in a multiplication problem.

Note that the missing-value problem in figure 3.4 includes two possible rates, cost per 1 bag of candy and number of bags of candy for $1. A common error that students make is to use the wrong unit rate. Students need experience interpreting each possible unit rate embedded in a task and determining which rate is appropriate to use in answering the question. Students should become accustomed to judging the reasonableness of their answers to decide whether they in fact used the correct unit rate. Students might solve unit-rate problems by generating two possible solutions—one from each unit rate—and then judging which answer is more reasonable. Often students solve the problem by using a calculator and generating two possible solutions with the two unit rates, and then they judge which answer is more reasonable. The activity Using a Unit Rate to Solve Problems, which appears later in this chapter, presents a series of unit-rate problems and gives you an opportunity to extend and refine your students' skills with proportionality.

The activities in this chapter, as in the rest of the book, are organized to allow the students first to develop, and then to present and share, their ideas. The discussions that follow give you opportunities to help the students build on their observations and solidify their understanding of the mathematics.

What Might Students Already Know about These Ideas?

Students enter middle school with many experiences dealing with multiplication and division. In third grade, students usually learn to solve one-step multiplication and division story problems that are in fact simple proportional reasoning tasks. By the middle grades, students should be able to build on their solutions for simple multiplication and division problems to solve more complex proportional reasoning tasks.

The first activity in chapter 3, Buying Pizza, presents students with a situation and a variety of problems. Activities like this can enable you to determine your students' level of understanding and their ability to apply it to proportional situations.

Buying Pizza

Goals

- Assess students' ability to apply their prior experience with and understanding of mathematics to proportional reasoning problems
- Foster students' experiences with and understanding of proportional reasoning

Materials

For each student—

- A copy of the blackline master "Buying Pizza"

For each pair of students—

- A sheet of chart paper

p. 131

Activity

Distribute a copy of the blackline master "Buying Pizza" to each student. Three problems ask the students to consider numbers of people and pizzas to think about proportions and rates. Have the students work individually at first, and then give them time to solve the three problems with a partner. Move around the room, coaching, asking questions, and noting particular strategies that you want to be sure that students share during follow-up large-group presentations. Have the students record their strategies on chart paper and present them in front of the class. During the students' presentations, ask questions as needed to clarify the students' thinking for others and to help the students make connections among strategies. Keep the strategies for future reference as the students explore the other proportionality activities in this chapter.

Discussion

Your students will probably generate a number of strategies for solving the three problems. Watch how they apply their understanding and note where they might need help before moving on to other proportional situations. The following examples and discussion come from the experiences of a teacher and her students in an actual sixth-grade classroom. Although your experience will probably be different, learning how this process worked in another class may give you ideas for how to assess and support your students' thinking.

Figure 3.6 shows how four sixth-grade students approached question 1 (the figure includes the question). Although the students in the class used a variety of strategies, Fayo's and Mohamed's solution strategies were the most common. By using strategies like Fayo's and Mohamed's, the students generated more data than they did with other strategies. However, their written work did not show whether they used repeated addition or multiplication to determine the number of pizzas. The class discussion gave the students a chance to describe their thinking. Most of the students who solved the problem the way Fayo and Mohamed

1. Ms. Carson plans to order pizza for a class party. She thinks that 4 pizzas will be enough for 10 people. Counting students and parent helpers, she needs to order enough pizza for 40 people. How many pizzas should she order? Describe your strategy.

Fayo's solution	Mohamed's solution
16 pizza. Because she need 4 pizza For every 10 people 4=10 8=20 12=30 16=40	Peppro | 80 | 30 | 40 | PiTT4 | 8 | 12 | 16 | Ms. Carson will have to order 16 Pizza
Marcus's solution	Ilsa's solution
(pizza drawings) = 40	4 ÷ 10 = 0.4 0.4 × 40 16.0 16 pizzas

did added corresponding amounts. For example, they said, "If I add 10 more people, then I add 4 more pizzas." Those students were able to generate data in this way to determine how many pizzas were needed for 40 people. A few students explained that they extended the data by multiplying 4 by 2 and 10 by 2, 4 by 3 and 10 by 3, and so on, often using the terms *double* and *triple*. The teacher asked questions to help the students see the similarity between multiplying and adding equal amounts.

As shown in figure 3.6, Marcus drew a picture to solve the problem. Marcus's picture showed that each group of 4 pizzas corresponded to 10 people. Questions posed by the teacher helped the students see that this picture could also be viewed as multiplication (4 times as many people; 4 times as many pizzas).

Ilsa used a unit-rate approach, also shown in figure 3.6. She divided 4 by 10 to determine the number of pizzas for one person, and then she multiplied that amount by 40 people to determine that 16 pizzas were needed. The students using the unit rate seemed unsure of where to place the decimal point in their calculations. However, they determined the correct answer, perhaps by judging what would be reasonable.

The students who used a repeated addition strategy to solve question 1 had to adapt their strategies for question 2, which changes the numbers from question 1 slightly. Ms. Carson thinks that 4 slightly larger pizzas will feed 16 people. How many of these pizzas would she need to serve 40 people? The quantity 40 is not a multiple of 16. Figure 3.7 shows some of the students' strategies for dealing with this slightly more complex situation. Starting with 4 pizzas for 16 people, Asha found two new data points: 2 pizzas for 8 people and 8 pizzas for 32 people. To find the number of pizzas for 40 people, she explained that she added 8 pizzas and 2 pizzas because 8 people and 32 people equaled 40 people. KiNoy's solution reflected multiplicative thinking (multiplying by $2\frac{1}{2}$) even though his explanation of what he did was in the language of addition.

Sylvia's approach was similar to KiNoy's. Sylvia's picture also shows the idea of multiplying the number of pizzas by $2\frac{1}{2}$, although she did not explain what she did in terms of multiplication, either. She noted

2. The pizzas at Grande's Pizza are really large. Ms. Carson thinks that 4 pizzas will be enough for 16 people. How many pizzas should she order for the 40 people at the class party?

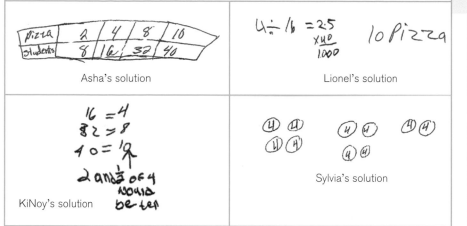

Asha's solution

Lionel's solution

KiNoy's solution

Sylvia's solution

Fig. **3.7.**

Students' solution strategies for question 2 on the "Buying Pizza" activity sheet

that each pizza represented 4 people and thus each group of 4 pizzas represented 16 people. She drew two sets of 4 pizzas and 1/2 of a set of 4 pizzas to correspond to 40 people. More students used a unit-rate strategy in this problem than in question 1. As in question 1, students like Lionel used the unit rate and placed the decimal point imprecisely during their calculations but reported a correct answer.

The students gave the fewest correct answers for question 3, which appears in figure 3.8. Probably the students encountered difficulty because no integer relationships exist either *within* or *across* the problem's measure spaces. Rather, the number of pizzas is increased by a factor of 1.5, and the number of pizzas needed per person is equal to $0.6\overline{6}$.

Some students reduced 4 : 6, the rate given, to 2 : 3 and then built a table to show other values up to the needed amount. Ravy's solution showed that she multiplied to generate the needed data pair, 6 : 9. Enrique appears to have done the same thing though his thinking was not evident in his written description of his strategy. A few students

3. At Broadway Pizza, 4 small pizzas are enough for 6 people. At this rate, for how many people will 6 pizzas be enough?

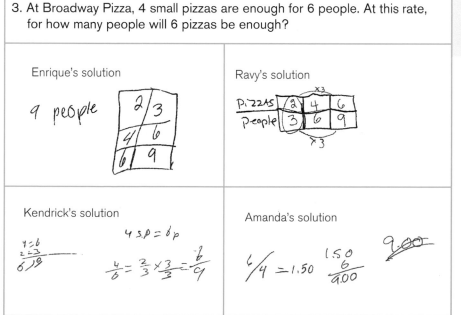

Enrique's solution

Ravy's solution

Kendrick's solution

Amanda's solution

Fig. **3.8.**

Students' solution strategies for question 3 on the "Buying Pizza" activity sheet

recorded problem information in fraction form for question 3—the only question for which they did so. For example, Kendrick's solution reflected thinking about fractions. He reduced the fraction 4/6 to 2/3, and then multiplied both numerator and denominator by 3 to find an equivalent fraction. Question 3 prompted more students to use a unit-rate strategy (like Amanda's solution in fig. 3.8) than did the other questions. However, a few students solved the problem incorrectly because they did not use the correct unit rate—number of people per pizza. Using the incorrect unit rate is a common misunderstanding among students using this strategy to solve proportional problems.

Another common misunderstanding of students involves the inappropriate use of the equal sign, as seen in Fayo's, KiNoy's, and Kendrick's solutions (figs. 3.6, 3.7, and 3.8, respectively). Fennell and Rowan (2001) stress that early misuse of the symbol, as in "16 = 4," may "hamper the leap into later mathematics because advancing in mathematics requires a more complete understanding of equations and equality" (p. 291). The fact that several students in this class used the equal sign inappropriately serves as a reminder that it is important to be sensitive to students' thinking and essential to work with them to ensure that they interpret and use symbols in a mathematically correct way.

The sixth-grade students' solutions to these problems show that students in the middle grades can employ a variety of ways to solve missing-value problems. The most common strategies relied on repeated addition or doubling, tripling, and so forth. Though some students needed pictures to work through the problems, a few showed that they were already thinking multiplicatively by using unit rates to solve the problems. Some students' strategies changed from problem to problem as the numerical characteristics changed. You can learn a lot about what your students already know about solving proportional reasoning tasks by using similar problems and by varying the numerical aspects of the problems. Listen to and observe the students' strategies, and give them time to consider the approaches of other students.

One way to foster the development of your students' mathematical power is to base your instruction on the ways that individual students solve problems. For example, the teacher of the class described above built on the unit-rate approach shared by a few students by developing new problems and asking all the students to try this approach.

Selected Instructional Activities

The remaining activities in this chapter emphasize building on various aspects of proportional thinking to help students develop an understanding of the mathematical characteristics of proportional situations. The activities also allow students to examine different types of problems, develop a qualitative understanding of rates, and develop unit-rate strategies.

As you begin exploring these ideas of proportionality with your students, remember that proportional reasoning is a theme that integrates many mathematical topics. Thus, you can find additional sources for

Post, Behr, and Lesh (1988) describe proportionality as a "convenient and perhaps necessary bridge between common numerical experiences and patterns and the more abstract relationships that will be expressed in algebraic form" (p. 80).

comparing and contrasting proportional and nonproportional problems in other areas of mathematics. For example, in the area of measurement, the relationships between units of measure provide one such context. Although conversions from inches to centimeters are proportional, conversions from Celsius to Fahrenheit temperatures are not.

Proportional reasoning is also important in the learning of algebra. Post, Behr, and Lesh (1988) describe three algebraic contexts (pp. 80-81):

- The algebraic representation of proportionality ($y = mx$) represents an "incredibly large class" of physical occurrences.

- Proportions expressed as two equivalent ratios are useful in a wide variety of problem-solving situations, such as many types of rate problems.

- Proportional situations provide an excellent vehicle to illustrate the multiple representations—tables, graphs, symbols (equations), pictures, and diagrams—that provide the conceptual underpinning for algebraic thinking.

Consider these connections as your students explore proportionality, and look for connections to proportionality as they explore other topics. The next three activities—Exchanging Currency; Pledge Drive; and Comparing Tables, Rules, and Graphs—are designed to help students discover the characteristics of proportional situations by giving them opportunities to compare proportional and nonproportional situations. Students also use their knowledge of linear functions to identify characteristics of proportional situations. After these activities, the activity Changing Rates encourages students to examine problem types. The final activity, Using a Unit Rate to Solve Problems, emphasizes helping students develop a unit-rate strategy.

Chapter 3 of *Navigating through Algebra in Grades 6–8* (Friel et al. 2001, pp. 37–58) offers suggestions for exploring linear functions with words, tables, graphs, and symbols. In those activities, students associate linearity with a constant rate of change between two variables and explore slope and *y*-intercept. Students can in turn use these ideas as tools to learn about proportionality and in so doing make connections among mathematical topics. After identifying proportional linear relationships in the activities in this book, students might usefully examine the linear functions in *Navigating through Algebra in Grades 6–8* to determine which ones represent proportional contexts.

Exchanging Currency

Goal

- Identify characteristics of proportional relationships by examining—
  - patterns in a table;
  - function rules; and
  - a graph.

Materials

For each student—

- A copy of the blackline master "Exchanging Currency"
- A copy of the blackline master "Centimeter Grid Paper"
- A graphing calculator (or access to a computer with spreadsheet software for each group of students; optional)

pp. 132–33; 134

Activity

Begin the activity Exchanging Currency by asking the students whether they have visited or lived in another country, and if so, what was the currency? Discuss the names of different currencies used around the world. If possible, bring to class samples of foreign currencies and a table from a newspaper or the Internet showing current exchange rates. Explain that when people exchange dollars for pounds, euros, or some other unit of currency, they are unlikely to be making a one-for-one exchange. Different currencies have different values relative to one another, determining different rates of exchange. Also emphasize that each rate of exchange fluctuates, so someone who exchanges dollars for pounds today may not get the same number of pounds that he or she would have gotten yesterday.

Distribute copies of the blackline master "Exchanging Currency." The activity sheet compares dollars (either U.S. or Canadian) to British pounds, but you can easily modify the sheet to compare other currencies. To make the computations relatively straightforward, the exchange rate in this activity is 3 dollars ($) for 2 pounds (£).

Have the students work in small groups to complete the activity sheet. It might be helpful for you to review the questions with the class to ensure that the students understand them. For your reference, figure 3.9 shows the table that the students complete before answering question 1, as well as the graph that they make in question 7. If you have electronic tools available, have the students use graphing calculators or a computer spreadsheet program to graph the values for question 7.

Once the students have completed the activity, discuss as a class the patterns that they found in the table. Have the students explain how they completed the table and used it to help them create rules relating the rates of exchange. To conclude the activity, you could compare the students' graph for question 7 with a graph showing the *current rate* of exchange.

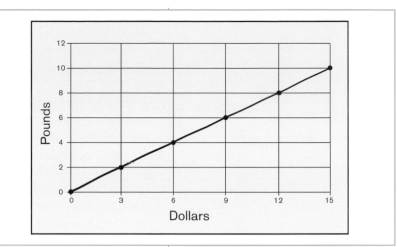

Dollars	Pounds
$3.00	£2.00
$6.00	£4.00
$9.00	£6.00
$12.00	£8.00
$15.00	£10.00
$18.00	£12.00

Fig. **3.9.**

The completed table showing dollars and pounds and the graph showing the number of pounds for any given number of dollars

Discussion

Your students are likely to employ a variety of strategies to complete the table. The explanations that they give of their work in question 1 and the patterns that they note in question 2 will also differ. In one eighth-grade class, a student summed up the most common strategy: "The dollars go up by threes and the pounds go up by twos. So I just counted by twos to figure out pounds." However, looking at the growth of the two variables is just one way of finding the corresponding number of pounds for a given number of dollars.

You should also expect some students to look at the functional relationships between variables to complete the data table. Students will probably approach the relationships in different ways. For example, one eighth grader noticed that she could find the number of pounds by subtracting 1/3 of the number of dollars from the total number of dollars. Another student stated, "Two pounds for 3 dollars is 2/3, so I found 2/3 of each number." Other students noted that dividing the number of dollars by 3 and multiplying by 2 would give the number of pounds. These functional relationships are equivalent, and when they arise during the class discussion (either in the students' observations or in your own), you can use the opportunity to help the students see how they are equal.

The students are likely to construct different strategies in question 3 for finding the corresponding amounts for $150 in pounds and for £16 in dollars. Many students will probably employ the straightforward and easy strategy of extending the table to find the corresponding dollar value for £16. But extending the table to find the number of pounds equivalent to $150 is more cumbersome. Thus, students will probably use a functional relationship (even if they haven't used one for other parts of the activity) to find the number of pounds equal to $150. Two typical strategies include (1) multiplying 150 by the fraction 2/3 and (2) making a two-step calculation: 150 ÷ 3 = 50, and 50 × 2 = 100.

You can expect the different approaches that the students use to change $150 to £100 to be mirrored in their answers to questions 4 and 5, when they write the two function rules to define the relationships between pounds and dollars. The students will probably write different expressions for determining the number of pounds to exchange for any

"Electronic technologies— calculators and computers—are essential tools for teaching, learning, and doing mathematics. They furnish visual images of mathematical ideas, they facilitate organizing and analyzing data, and they compute efficiently and accurately.... When technological tools are available, students can focus on decision making, reflection, reasoning, and problem solving."
(NCTM 2000, p. 24)

given number of dollars. For example, some eighth graders displayed the relationship as a fraction, $p = (2/3)d$, or as decimal multiplication, $p \approx (0.666)d$. Other students depicted the relationship with one of three operator interpretations for fraction multiplication: $p = (d \div 3) \times 2$, $p = (d \times 2) \div 3$, or $p = (2 \times d)/3$. Common expressions of a rule to determine the number of dollars for any given number of pounds included $d \approx p \div 0.66$, $d = p \div 2/3$, $d = (1.5)p$, $d = (3/2)p$, $d = (p \div 2) \times 3$, and $d = (3p)/2$. Some students interpreted the relationship as fraction (or decimal) multiplication or division, and others saw it in terms of an operator—multiply or divide first, and then divide or multiply. Building connections among the different rules is important. Much of your teaching will occur after your students have presented their ideas, giving you an opportunity to build on their observations to make the mathematics explicit.

In question 6, the students must use their rules to convert pounds to dollars and dollars to pounds. Ask your students how they determined which rule to use; in part (*a*) the rule is $d = (3/2)p$, and in part (*b*) the rule is $p = (2/3)d$. Focus the students' attention on the reasonableness of their answers.

For question 7, ask the students to show and explain their graphs for $p = (2/3)d$. The class discussion should elicit the facts that the graph is a straight line, its slope is positive, and it goes through the origin. Ask the students why the line passes through the origin.

The students analyze this scenario further in the activity Comparing Tables, Rules, and Graphs later in this chapter. Collect and save the students' work on Exchanging Currency (or ask them to save it) so that they can refer to it in that later activity.

In the next activity, Pledge Drive, the students examine the same types of features as they did in Exchanging Currency, but this time the situation is not proportional.

Pledge Drive

Goal

- Identify characteristics of nonproportional linear relationships by examining—
  - patterns in a table;
  - function rules; and
  - a graph.

Materials

For each student—

- A copy of the blackline master "Pledge Drive"
- A graphing calculator (or access to a computer with spreadsheet software for each group of students; optional)

pp. 135–37

Activity

Distribute a copy of the blackline master "Pledge Drive" to each student. In this activity, the students examine the relationship between the number of kilometers and the amount of money that Andrea raises for a charity. Andrea's sponsors pledge $1.50 plus $0.50 for each kilometer that she travels on her bike. As in the activity Exchanging Currency, the students complete a table, examine relationships in the table, discover and apply rules, and create a graph for one of the rules.

Have the students work in small groups to complete the activity sheet. Figure 3.10 shows the completed table as well as the graph that the students make in question 7. If possible, have the students use graphing calculators or a computer spreadsheet to graph the values for question 7. As the students become more comfortable with their ability to generate

Fig. 3.10.

The completed table showing kilometers and money pledged and the graph showing the number of dollars for any given number of kilometers

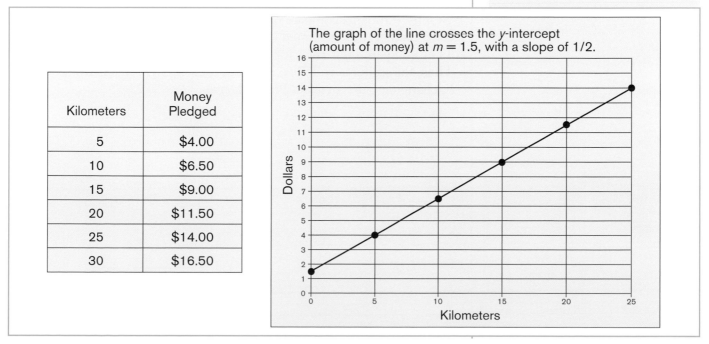

Kilometers	Money Pledged
5	$4.00
10	$6.50
15	$9.00
20	$11.50
25	$14.00
30	$16.50

The graph of the line crosses the y-intercept (amount of money) at $m = 1.5$, with a slope of 1/2.

tables or graphs of functions electronically, they will be prepared to use these tools to focus on the general nature of functions. Although they are limited here to identifying the characteristics of proportional and nonproportional linear relationships, students will later extend these electronic explorations to nonlinear situations.

Once the students have finished the activity, discuss how they completed the table and what patterns they found in the data. Discuss the answers to the rest of the activity sheet, being sure to highlight and make connections among the students' various approaches.

Discussion

Although the activities Exchanging Currency and Pledge Drive are organized in a similar manner and ask similar questions, the students might very well approach the two data tables in different ways. Eighth graders who completed both activities constructed the data tables differently. To complete the table in Exchanging Currency, they depended on the growth patterns that they observed in the table. However, for Pledge Drive, they used the functional relationship between the two variables. One student described the relationship in this way, "I multiplied the kilometers by $0.50 and then added $1.50." To the students, the rule for these data might have been more obvious than the rule for the data in Exchanging Currency. This difference might explain why the majority of the class used the pattern that the student described to complete the data table.

Be sure to discuss with your students the different strategies that they used. Expect them to be flexible in how they solve the problems because the numerical aspects of the task are likely to affect their strategies. If they chose different strategies from one activity to the next, have them explain why. Save the students' completed activity sheets for reference in the next activity.

At this point, your students should be ready to use their knowledge of linear functions to look more closely at what is special about proportional situations. In the next activity—Comparing Tables, Rules, and Graphs—students compare patterns in the tables representing the contexts that they examined in Exchanging Currency and Pledge Drive. They compare their rules for the two situations as well as their graphs. Thus, the students will need access to their activity sheets from both Exchanging Currency and Pledge Drive.

Comparing Tables, Rules, and Graphs

Goal

- Distinguish proportional relationships from nonproportional relationships by comparing
  - patterns in tables;
  - function rules; and
  - graphs.

Materials

For each student—

- A copy of the blackline master "Poring over the Patterns"
- A copy of the blackline master "Getting a Grip on the Graphs"
- A copy of the blackline master "Proposing a Proportional Plan"
- The student's completed copies of the blackline masters "Exchanging Currency" and "Pledge Drive"
- A graphing calculator (or access to a computer with spreadsheet software for each group of students; optional)

pp. 138–44

Activity

Distribute a copy of the activity sheet for part 1, "Poring over the Patterns," to each student, and place the students in small groups. In this part of the activity, the students review the data from the activities Exchanging Currency and Pledge Drive. They compare the patterns that they observed in the data sets as well as the rules that they wrote to describe them. Ask the students to work in their groups to complete part 1. Point out that they will need to refer to their work on the previous activity sheets, "Exchanging Currency" and "Pledge Drive." While the students work, move among the groups and ask students to explain their answers to some of the questions. These conversations should help you determine how to focus the class discussion.

Once the students have finished part 1, have the class discuss the two tables and the rules (see fig. 3.11). Discuss the students' answers to questions 1–6 of part 1, focusing on strategies as well as misconceptions from the students' earlier work in their small groups. Help the students make connections between the patterns in the tables and the rules.

Next, distribute copies of the activity sheet for part 2, "Getting a Grip on the Graphs." In this part of the activity, the students make two graphs. The first is for $p = (2/3)d$, the rule for finding the number of pounds (p) in terms of the number of dollars (d) in Exchanging Currency. The second graph is for $m = (0.5)k + 1.5$, the rule for finding the amount of money (m) that a sponsor pledges to give Andrea in terms of the number of kilometers (k) that she rides on her bicycle in Pledge Drive. The students compare and describe the graphs. Have the students complete part 2 and discuss as a class their observations about their graphs. To complete the graphs, the students can use the included grids,

Exchanging Currency		Pledge Drive	
Dollars	Pounds	Kilometers	Money Raised
$3.00	£2.00	5	$4.00
$6.00	£4.00	10	$6.50
$9.00	£6.00	15	$9.00
$12.00	£8.00	20	$11.50
$15.00	£10.00	25	$14.00
$18.00	£12.00	30	$16.50

$d = (3/2)p$ or $p = (2/3)d$, where d = the number of dollars and p = the number of pounds

$k = (m - 1.5)/0.5$ or $m = (0.5)k + 1.5$, where k = the number of kilometers and m = the amount of money

or if graphing calculators or computers with spreadsheet software are available, the students can use those tools. If any group uses graphing calculators or spreadsheets to complete part 2, you might have the students demonstrate how they used these electronic tools.

After the class discusses part 2 and the students develop an understanding of the characteristics of proportional situations (see the "Discussion" section below), distribute copies of the activity sheet for part 3, "Proposing a Proportional Plan." In this part of the activity, the students devise a proportional system for Andrea's fund-raising. They develop a table, a rule, and a graph that show a proportional relationship between the amount of money (m) that a sponsor pledges and the number of kilometers (k) that Andrea rides on her bike. Have the students complete and discuss part 3.

Discussion

As the class discusses part 1, "Poring over the Patterns," the students should note the following patterns in the Exchanging Currency table and realize that analogous patterns are not present in the Pledge Drive table:

- Doubling the number of dollars doubles the number of pounds, tripling the number of dollars triples the number of pounds, and so on.
- The rates (pounds/dollars) for the data are 2/3, 4/6, 6/9. They are all equivalent to 2/3.
- The reciprocal rates (dollars/pounds) all equal 3/2.
- The two rules for the data are $p = (2/3)d$ and $d = (3/2)p$, where d represents the number of dollars and p represents the number of pounds. The factors defining the relationships between pounds and dollars (2/3 and 3/2) are the constant rates found in the table.

Once the students have completed part 2 of the activity, have them share their comparisons of the graphs (shown in fig. 3.12) in a class discussion. Focus particularly on what they noticed about the y-intercepts

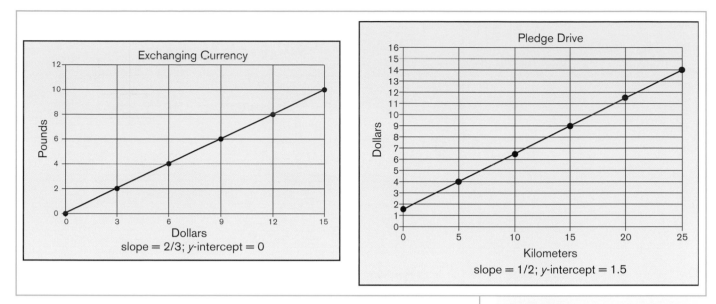

Fig. **3.12.**

Graphs of data from Exchanging Currency and Pledge Drive

and slopes. The students should recognize that although both graphs are linear, the *y*-intercepts differ. Ask the students to explain why one line crosses the *y*-axis at the origin and the other has a *y*-intercept of 1.5. Help them connect the rules that they wrote with the context for each situation.

Ask the students to describe the connection between the slopes of the lines and the rules. The students should notice that although the slopes of the lines for both graphs correspond to the coefficient of their respective rule, the slope of the line $p = (2/3)d$ is one of the constant rates found in the Exchanging Currency table (and the reciprocal of the slope is the other rate from the table).

Point out to your students that the Exchanging Currency data illustrate a special linear function—a direct proportion. Turn the students' attention to the differences between the situations in Exchanging Currency and Pledge Drive. Ask them to explain what they think is special about direct proportions. They should recognize that the relationship between the two quantities in a direct proportion is defined only by multiplication or division. The students should also realize that in a direct proportion, the patterns in the table and the special features of the graph exist because the relationship between quantities involves only multiplication or division.

Now ask the students to complete part 3 of the activity, which asks them to adjust Andrea's fund-raising system in Pledge Drive to make it proportional. Give the students time to present their new systems for pledges and to support their claims of proportionality by pointing out patterns in the table and special features in the graph and the rule.

Eighth graders who completed this activity as well as the previous two activities usually realized that they needed only to drop the addition of $1.50 to make the situation proportional. Most of the students also decided to change the amount charged for each kilometer. Ted's work, shown in figure 3.13, is an example of this approach. Although Ted supported his belief that the changed context was now proportional with his rule and graph, he did not note patterns in the table. Ted's teacher took the opportunity to ask questions to help Ted and others in

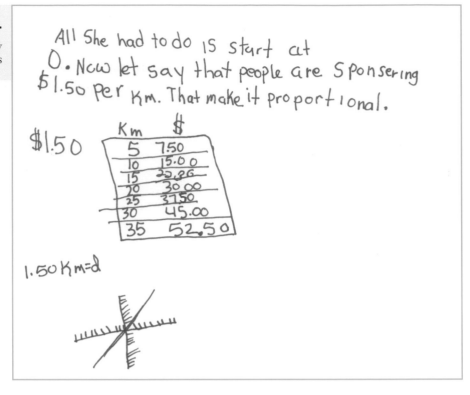

the class focus on the patterns and the constant rates to give additional support to Ted's new assertion that his system was proportional.

You can conclude the discussion by asking your students to describe other real-world situations that are proportional and others that are not. This exercise will help your students cement their thinking about what makes a relationship proportional.

The next activity, Changing Rates, helps students explore another aspect of proportional reasoning by having them solve problems involving qualitative prediction. These problems challenge students to think about the quantities involved and the relationships among them. The activity asks students to consider different ways in which changes in the quantities making up a rate affect the rate. The students also construct a table to organize their generalizations about how a rate changes when parts of it change.

Changing Rates

Goal

- Determine the effect of changing the numerator or the denominator (or both) on the rate embedded in a story problem

Materials

For each student—

- A copy of the blackline master "Changing Rates"

For each group of four students—

- An 11-by-17-inch sheet of paper
- Scissors
- Markers
- A roll of transparent tape

pp. 145–46

Activity

Distribute a copy of the blackline master "Changing Rates" to each student, and then place the students in groups of four. Give each group a large sheet of paper and scissors, markers, and tape. Explain that each of the eight problems on the activity sheet involves a rate (a fixed ratio between two quantities). Tell the students that they will need to consider the information in each problem and determine the rate. They will also have to decide whether the changes described in each problem increase the rate, decrease it, or keep it the same—or whether they do not have enough information to know if or how the rate has changed.

Problems from the "Changing Rates" Activity Sheet

Problem 1: Josie noticed that the cost of bags of candy at the whole-sale club changed from last week. Today she paid more money for fewer bags of candy. How did the cost per bag change?

Problem 2: The London Bank gave more British pounds in exchange for the same number of U.S. dollars this week than it did last week. Did the exchange rate, £/$, increase, decrease, or stay the same—or can't you tell?

Problem 3: Marta rides her bike every morning. She keeps track of the distance and time that she rides. Today she traveled a greater distance and rode a longer time than she did yesterday. How did her speed change?

Problem 4: Rodrigo has a recipe for making lemonade. He mixes some lemonade concentrate with some water. He decides to change the recipe, decreasing the amount of lemonade concentrate and increasing the amount of water. Does the lemonade taste stronger, weaker, or the same—or can't you tell?

Problem 5: Today the London Bank gave fewer British pounds in exchange for fewer U.S. dollars than it did yesterday. Did the exchange rate, £/$, increase, decrease, or stay the same—or can't you tell?

Problem 6: Thomas rode his bike the same distance today as yesterday, but today he took a longer time. Did his speed increase, decrease, or stay the same—or can't you tell?

Problem 7: Rodrigo changed his lemonade mixture again. This time he kept the amount of lemonade concentrate the same as in his new recipe in problem 4 but decreased the amount of water. What happened to the taste of his new lemonade compared with the taste of the lemonade he created in problem 4? Did the new lemonade taste stronger, weaker, or the same—or can't you tell?

Problem 8: Josie paid less money today than she did yesterday for the same number of bags of candy. How did the cost per bag change?

To ensure that your students understand how to approach the activity, have them examine problem 1 as a class. After the students read the problem, discuss how they might sort out the information and determine whether this rate has changed. Ask questions such as the following, and encourage the students to ask themselves similar questions as they look at the other problems (answers for problem 1 are in parentheses):

- "What is the rate that you have to consider in this problem? State it in words." (Cost for one bag)
- "How can we write that rate as a relationship *a/b*?" (Cost/bag)
- "What changes has the rate undergone? Has one quantity changed or have both changed?" (The cost, or the numerator, has increased, and the number of bags, or the denominator, has decreased—both quantities are changing.)
- "Can you draw a picture to show how the rate changes?" (Fig. 3.14 shows two sample illustrations.)
- "Imagine that you have to pay more for fewer bags of candy. This is what Josie had to do. Are you paying more now for *each* bag, less, or the same amount as before—or is it not possible to tell?" (More for each bag) "How can you explain your answer to your neighbor so she or he understands?"
- "Does thinking about the cost for one bag of candy help you think through this problem? If so, how?" (If each bag costs more, then the value of the rate increases.)

Next, have the students work in their groups to analyze each problem on the activity sheet. After they have identifed the rate, the changes to each quantity in the rate (the numerator and denominator), and how they think the rate has changed in each case, have them cut out the problems from one group member's activity pages. Ask them to sort the problems into the following categories, which you should also post on

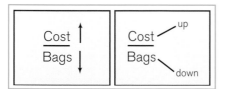

Fig. **3.14.**

Two illustrations of the rate change in problem 1

the board: "Rate Increases," "Rate Decreases," "Rate Stays the Same," and "Cannot Tell." Tell the students to write these categories on the sheet of paper that you have given them, and have them loosely tape each problem in the appropriate category.

Match each group of students with one other group and have the groups explain to each other why they classified the problems as they did. After the discussion, the groups can change their classifications of the problems if they wish. Give all the groups time to discuss the generalizations that they can make about rates.

Discussion

Begin the class discussion of the activity by calling for volunteers to tell which rates have increased. Ask the students to explain why they think so. Go through all the categories in this manner. As the discussion unfolds, you might want to ask the class some or all of the following questions:

- "What rate is embedded in the problem? What does the rate mean?"
- "What change does the rate undergo? Why do you think that change has occurred?" (See fig. 3.15.)

Problem	Rate	Changes in Numerator	Changes in Denominator
1	cost/bags	↑	↓
2	pounds/dollars	↑	—
3	distance/time	↑	↑
4	lemonade concentrate/water	↓	↑
5	pounds/dollars	↓	↓
6	distance/time	—	↑
7	lemonade concentrate/water	—	↓
8	cost/bags	↑	—

Fig. **3.15.**

The rates and changes in the numerator and denominator for each problem in Changing Rates. An increase is marked by an up arrow, a decrease is marked by a down arrow, and no change is marked by a horizontal line segment.

- "What were some of the disagreements that you had initially with the other group when you shared how you categorized the problems?"
- "How did you reconcile these disagreements?"
- "Does any group have a different way to explain why the rates in this category change as they do?"
- "Does any group disagree with this group's categorization?"

When the students have reached a consensus on the problems that belong in a category, record the problem numbers on the board. Repeat the process until the students have agreed on problems in all four categories. Figure 3.16 shows the categories and the problems.

Fig. **3.16.**

How the rate in each problem changed

Rate Increases	Rate Decreases	Rate Stays the Same	Cannot Tell
Problem 1	Problem 4		Problem 3
Problem 2	Problem 6		Problem 5
Problem 7	Problem 8		

Your students will probably have varying degrees of success in categorizing the rate changes. Although none of the eight problems falls into the "stays the same" category, you can expect some students to suggest that the rates in problems 3 and 5 do not change. A rate stays the same if the quantities in the rate have not changed or if the changes are proportional. Students might reason that the rates in problems 3 and 5 stay the same because both the numerator and denominator change in the same direction. But this reasoning overlooks the fact that the problems do not specify by how much the quantities change. If both quantities in a rate increase proportionally (that is, by the same factor), then the rate will stay the same. If the quantities in a rate change in a nonproportional way (that is, by different factors or by adding an amount to each), the rate will not stay the same. Because the students do not know whether the quantities in problems 3 and 5 change proportionally, they cannot determine how the rates change.

The context in which this type of rate change is embedded might affect the students' ability to recognize when they cannot predict the change in the rate. One seventh-grade student, Tara, struggled with problems 3 and 5 in the activity. She concluded that the rate in problem 3, distance/time, does not change, since both distance and time increased. She tested her theory with a numerical example:

$$15 \text{ miles}/15 \text{ minutes} = 30 \text{ miles}/30 \text{ minutes}.$$

Because both rates reduce to 1 mile/1 minute, Tara concluded that increasing both quantities does not change the rate. In her numerical example, Tara increased both the quantities proportionally (by a factor of 2). Likewise, in problem 5, she concluded (incorrectly) that since the two quantities, pounds and dollars, both decrease, the rate decreases.

Because Tara reasoned incorrectly on both problems, her teacher asked her a similar question framed in a more familiar context. The teacher asked Tara how the taste of lemonade would change if someone changed the recipe by decreasing both the lemonade concentrate and the water. Tara quickly said that she could not tell because she did not know by how much the lemonade concentrate and water had been decreased. She was able to give examples in which decreasing both lemonade mix and water would make stronger lemonade and in which decreasing both quantities would make weaker lemonade. Her personal experience with lemonade might have enabled her to reason correctly about this situation though she was unable to think through problems 3 and 5.

Eventually, you'll want your students to have flexible reasoning skills that they can apply to familiar and unfamiliar situations alike. But for now, you might want to turn to familiar situations to help students solidify their skills with these new and more complex concepts of proportionality. If your students struggle with problems 3 and 5, familiar contexts may help them see that when the quantities in a rate change in the same direction but the amount of change is not specified, then the students cannot conclude that the rate stays the same.

During the activity, the students should have started to make generalizations about how changes in the two quantities that make up a rate affect the rate. To conclude the activity, discuss those generalizations, and work as a class to sum them up. You can create a chart similar to the one in figure 3.17. You can use words ("stays the same," "increases," or "decreases") or symbols (a horizontal line segment, an upward arrow, or a downward arrow, respectively) to show the changes. As you discuss these generalizations, some students might need a familiar context to help them visualize the rate change. For example, to visualize an increase, you might suggest that the students think about a given cost per bag for bags of candy. If the numerator in the rate (the cost) increases and the denominator in the rate (the number of bags) remains the same, the rate (cost/bag) will increase.

Numerator / Denominator	—	↑	↓
—	Rate stays the same	Rate increases	Rate decreases
↑	Rate decreases	Cannot tell	Rate decreases
↓	Rate increases	Rate increases	Cannot tell

Fig. **3.17.**

A summary of how changes in the numerator, the denominator, or both affect the overall rate (a horizontal line represents no change, an up arrow represents an increase, and a down arrow represents a decrease)

In the final activity, Using a Unit Rate to Solve Problems, students find and interpret unit rates and use unit rates to solve missing-value problems.

Using a Unit Rate to Solve Problems

Goals

- Determine the two possible unit rates for a relationship
- Explain the meaning of the two identified unit rates
- Solve problems using a unit-rate strategy

Materials

For each student—

- A copy of the blackline master "Using a Unit Rate to Solve Problems "
- A calculator

pp. 147–49

Activity

This activity encourages the students to identify and apply unit rates that are embedded in problems. To introduce the activity, you might want to review with the students what they know about unit rates.

Start by asking the students what a unit rate describes. They should understand that a unit rate tells "how many for one" and is found through simple division. The unit rate always indicates how many units of the numerator "come with" one unit of the denominator. For example, the rate 60 miles in two hours equals the unit rate 30 miles per hour (30 miles / 1 hour).

Have the students brainstorm to create a list of unit rates from daily life. Some examples of such unit rates include 30 students for one teacher, $1.95 per pound of ground beef, $4.25 per ticket, and 12 eggs per dozen. Ask the students to explain the meaning of each unit rate that they suggest and how they could use the rate to answer related questions. Questions related to the examples above might include "How many teachers are needed for 90 students?" "How much do 3.5 pounds of ground beef cost?" "How much will 10 tickets cost?" and "How many eggs are in 5 dozen?"

Turn the discussion to how to identify a rate in an everyday situation. Say something like, "I can drive my car 600 miles with 20 gallons of gasoline." Ask the students to consider two possible ways to express the relationship between miles and gallons as a rate (600 miles/20 gallons or 20 gallons/600 miles). Discuss the meaning of these rates, using questions like the following (answers are in parentheses):

- "Why is it important to include the labels when writing rates?" (The meaning of the rate is lost without the labels.)
- "On average, how many miles can this car travel on one gallon of gas?" (30 miles/gallon)
- "How many gallons does this car need to travel one mile?" (1/30 gallon for one mile)
- "If I want to know the number of gallons I will need to drive 450 miles, what rate can I use? How?" ("Since I want to know

the number of gallons for 450 miles, I can use the rate 1/30 gallon per one mile and multiply by 450 miles: 1/30 gallon/mile × 450 miles = 15 gallons.")

- "What question might I ask that I would be likely to answer by using the other rate?" (For example, "My car holds 15 gallons of gasoline. How many miles can my car travel on one tank of gas?")

- "Show me how to answer your question by using the rate." ("Since I want to know the number of miles I can travel on 15 gallons, I can use the rate of 30 miles per one gallon and multiply by 15 gallons: 30 miles/gallon × 15 gallons = 450 miles.")

This scenario presents a good opportunity for you to help students distinguish between exact rates and approximate rates. Explain that although rates such as cost per ticket are exact, rates such as miles per gallon are built on averages and expectations of similar driving conditions. In reality, the number of gallons needed to drive one mile is likely to be much greater than the reciprocal of a car's average miles per gallon.

Next, distribute a copy of the activity sheet "Using a Unit Rate to Solve Problems" to each student, and have the students work in pairs or small groups to complete it. The activity sheet presents three situations with embedded rates (see the margin). As the students work, move around the room, asking them to explain the meaning of the rates. Remind the students that the unit rate tells "how many for one." Often, having the students use words to explain the meaning for a rate helps them determine which rate to use. Do not be surprised if students use both rates to solve the problems and then determine which of their two answers is reasonable in the context. This is frequently the initial way in which students use unit rates to solve problems.

Discussion

For the class discussion, call on volunteers to explain how they determined which unit rate to use to solve the problems in this activity. Then have the students share their work for problem 3(*d*), which asks them to write two questions that they would use unit rates to answer about the Martinez family's trip. You might want to encourage other students to try to answer those questions. Depending on the other experiences that the students have had, you might want to have them explore the connections between unit rates and proportional situations. They could look at how unit rates relate to patterns in data tables, slopes of graphs, and function rules for proportional situations.

To help the students consider the properties of proportional situations, ask them to solve the following problem (Rachlin and Preston 2001):

William ran around the school's track as fast as Sara. Sara started first. By the time Sara had run 9 laps, William had completed 3 laps. Sara ran 18 laps in all and stopped. William stopped then, too. How many laps did William finish? (Teacher's Guide 16, p. 5)

Do not be surprised if many students say that William ran 6 laps. Superficially, this problem features characteristics of a proportional missing-value problem. The problem presents three pieces of information and one unknown, and the context deals with running. However,

1. Marcus runs around the track every day after school. He believes that with practice he can be a track star. He can run 12 laps around the school's track in 30 minutes.

2. Michelle, an exchange student from France, will be in the United State for the next four months. In France, she buys everything with euros. When she came to the United States, she had to exchange her euros for U.S. dollars. She went to the bank and exchanged her money at the rate of 4.5 euros for 5 dollars.

3. The Martinez family is planning to drive from New York to Florida during winter break to visit the Kennedy Space Center. The scale on the map that they are using to plan their trip is 2.5 cm = 125 miles.

Sara	William
9	3
10	4
11	5
12	6
13	7
14	8
15	9
16	10
17	11
18	12

the quantities are not proportional. Thus, doubling 9 laps to get 18 laps and then doubling 3 laps to get the total number of William's laps will not give the correct answer. Finding a unit rate will not provide the answer, either. The unit-rate strategy (3 of William's laps to 9 of Sara's laps = 1/3 of a lap by William to 1 lap by Sara; $1/3 \times 18 = 6$) does not reflect the problem situation.

To help the students understand why the situation is not proportional, ask them to complete a table like the one in the margin. The students should understand that they can make such a table because Sara and William are running at the same speed—they simply started running at different times. Therefore, once they are running, the difference between their numbers of laps will always be the same. Each time Sara completes one lap, William also completes one lap. The data in the table show that the relationship between the number of laps that William runs and the number of laps that Sara runs is linear but not proportional.

The function rule for obtaining the number of William's laps (w) from the number of Sara's laps (s) is $w = s - 6$. Thus, when Sara stops running after 18 laps, William has completed 12 laps. The relationship between the two quantities is not proportional because it is not defined by multiplication. The students must learn that the strategies developed in tasks like those in the activities in this chapter will work only in proportional contexts.

Extensions

The following ideas and resources on the CD-ROM offer some alternative and additional ways for you to think about and approach the topics presented in this chapter.

Identifying Situations as Additive or Multiplicative

Put yourself in your students' shoes. Distinguishing when problem contexts are additive ($y = x + b$) and when they are multiplicative ($y = mx$) is challenging. So is determining when to measure the relationship between two quantities by finding a difference ($y - x = b$) and when to measure it by finding a ratio ($y/x = m$).

The following problem, given to prospective teachers in a methods course, together with samples of their solutions, can illustrate these challenges:

A new housing subdivision offers lots of three different sizes: 185 feet by 245 feet, 75 feet by 114 feet, and 455 feet by 508 feet. If you were to view these lots from above, which would appear to be the most square? Which would appear to be the least square? Explain your answers. (Marty Simon, personal communication, April 1997)

To compare the rectangular plots, many of the prospective teachers used the differences between the lengths and widths of the lots rather than the ratios of their lengths and widths. That is, they used the notion that the difference between the length and width of a square is 0, rather than that the ratio of the length and width of a square is 1. Consider the following three excerpts of the prospective teachers'

Navigating through Number and Operations in Grades 6–8

problem-solving approaches (Rachlin and Preston 2001, Teacher's Guide 12, "Writing Assignment").

The first solution serves as an example of a common incorrect argument that the preservice teachers offered for using the differences between the lengths:

> I drew diagrams for each of the three different possible plots of land. When a piece of land is listed as 185 feet by 245 feet, that means that the 2 lengths of the diagram are l85 feet and the 2 widths are 245 feet. Since a square has all 4 sides of equal length, it is obvious that none of the examples given are perfectly square. To find the ones that were most and least square, I found the difference between the two measurements for each plot of land. The one with the smallest difference is most square because it means that the 2 lengths are the closest in "feet" to the 2 widths. The one with the greatest difference is least square because it means that the 2 lengths are the farthest in "feet" to the 2 widths. Most square: 75 feet by 114 feet; least square, 185 feet by 245 feet.

The second solution uses ratios and differences. This preservice teacher first found the area of the plot and then found the ratio of the difference of the side lengths to the area:

$$185 \cdot 245 = 45325, \text{ and } 60/45325 = 0.0013237;$$
$$75 \text{ feet by } 114 \text{ feet} = 8550, \text{ and } 39/8550 = 0.0045614;$$
$$455 \cdot 508 = 231140, \text{ and } 53/231140 = 0.0002292;$$

> 455 feet by 508 feet is the most square (and the largest area). The ratio between the difference of the sides to the area is the smallest, or closest to 0.

This method works but is more elaborate than the third solution, which illustrates how some prospective teachers used ratios or other forms of multiplicative reasoning elegantly:

> [The plot that is most nearly square is] 455 feet by 508 feet. Why? Because $n \times n$ is a square … and that can be written n/n, which equals 1. When you divide the two measurements, the one closest to 1 is the most square—185/245 = 0.7551; 75/114 = 0.6579; 455/508 = 0.8957. 455 feet by 508 feet is the closest to 1.

Initially, the additive solution (the closer the difference of the sides is to 0, the closer the rectangular field is to square) appeared correct to many preservice teachers. However, they saw the inappropriateness of additive reasoning for these situations when they tried the next problem (Rachlin and Preston 2001), which holds the differences between the side lengths constant while the dimensions vary:

> The science club at Northridge Middle School is planting four separate rectangular plots as part of a horticultural experiment. One plot is 1 foot by 4 feet, a second is 7 feet by 10 feet, a third is 17 feet by 20 feet, and a fourth is 27 feet by 30 feet. Draw the plots on a centimeter grid and state which rectangle is the most square. Which rectangle is the least square? Explain your answers. (Teacher's Guide 14, p. 3)

On the CD-ROM, Miller and Fey (2000) and Langrall and Swafford (2000) present alternative ways to classify proportional-reasoning tasks.

These extended examples illustrate the challenges of deciding what type of reasoning to use to solve a problem. Be sensitive as your students struggle with similar situations, and look for ways to help them realize on their own when their reasoning is inappropriate for the task at hand.

Thinking about Proportional Reasoning

The articles on proportional reasoning on the CD-ROM offer both alternative problems for you to use with your students and alternative, but complementary, ways to reflect on the development of children's proportional reasoning.

In their article, Miller and Fey (2000) cite three processes that students use in approaching problems that embed proportions in authentic settings: "(1) recognizing when proportional thinking makes sense, (2) testing the equivalence of two or more ratios, and (3) solving proportional equations to find an unknown" (p. 312). The authors assert that proportional-reasoning tasks involve problem solvers in (a) "thinking about the relative size of two parts in some common whole," (b) comparing "different quantities that have an interesting relationship to each other … often expressed in the language of unit rates or densities," and (c) "reasoning about the similarities of figures … often expressed in the language of ratios of corresponding parts, or scale factors" (p. 312).

Langrall and Swafford (2000) provide a synthesis of their search of the literature on proportional reasoning. Drawing heavily on research by Susan Lamon (1999) and investigators from the Rational Number Project, they offer an alternative classification of four proportional reasoning problem types and four levels of strategies for proportional reasoning, along with their essential components of proportional reasoning (see fig. 3.18).

For more information about, and a bibliography for, the Rational Number Project, see the Web site education.umn.edu/ rationalnumberproject/.

Conclusion

The activities in chapter 3 have emphasized examining the characteristics of proportional situations by comparing data patterns, graphs, and function rules in proportional and nonproportional situations. The chapter has also offered ideas for different types of problems and varied samples of students' strategies.

The lessons in chapter 3 are examples of the types of problems and activities that students should experience to develop their proportional-reasoning skills. No activity in the chapter asks students to solve missing-value problems by setting up a proportion and using a standard cross-product algorithm. The activities seek to help students develop a deeper and more complex understanding of proportionality than they gain when they proceed directly to the learning of efficient algorithms for solving a single problem type.

In the middle grades, students need to approach proportionality from multiple perspectives over an extended period of time. Learning to reason proportionally is a complicated and time-consuming task. This chapter has attempted to capture some of that complexity.

Proportional-Reasoning Problem Types and Examples

Part-part-whole

Example: "Mrs. Jones put her students into groups of 5. Each group had 3 girls. If she has 25 students, how many girls and how many boys does she have in her class?"

Well-known measures

Example: "Dr. Day drove 156 miles and used 6 gallons of gasoline. At this rate, can he drive 561 miles on a full tank of 21 gallons of gasoline?"

Associated sets

Example: "Ellen, Jim, and Steve bought 3 helium-filled balloons and paid $2 for all 3 balloons. They decided to go back to the store and buy enough balloons for everyone in the class. How much did they pay for 24 balloons?"

Growth (stretching and shrinking situations)

Example: "A 6″ × 8″ photograph was enlarged so that the width changed from 8″ to 12″. What is the height of the new photograph?"

Levels of Strategies for Proportional Reasoning	Essential Components of Proportional Reasoning
Nonproportional reasoning (Level 0)	Recognize the difference between absolute (additive) and relative (multiplicative) change
Informal reasoning about proportional situations (Level 1)	Recognize situations where using a ratio is reasonable or appropriate
Quantitative reasoning (Level 2)	Understand that the quantities that make up a ratio covary in such a way that the relationship between them remains unchanged (is invariant)
Formal proportional reasoning (Level 3)	Build increasingly complex unit structures (unitize)

Fig. **3.18.**

Types of proportional reasoning problems and levels of strategies for proportional reasoning (and their essential components) (adapted from Langrall and Swafford 2000, pp. 255–59)

NAVIGATIONS
SERIES

GRADES 6–8

NAVIGATING *through* NUMBER *and* OPERATIONS

Looking Back and Looking Ahead

In the middle grades, students' experiences with concepts of number and operations should help them cross a bridge. That bridge takes them from their foundational and informal experiences with number concepts and reasoning in elementary school to formal and deductive experiences with algebra at the secondary level.

Each chapter in this book emphasizes the problem solving, reasoning, and thinking skills that students must develop to cross that bridge. These skills include (a) a deepening understanding of and facility with fractions, decimals, and percents; (b) an ability to visualize and conceptualize operations with rational numbers; (c) a facility and fluency with rational-number operations; (d) a flexibility in using multiple representations as tools for analysis and synthesis; and (e) an ability to investigate, interpret, and apply proportional reasoning as a multiplicative relationship. The activities, applets, and information in this book and on its accompanying CD-ROM are designed to help you facilitate your students' progress toward mathematical literacy and empowerment.

From their experiences in the middle grades, students should enter high school adding, subtracting, multiplying, and dividing integers, fractions, and decimals fluently. They should also be able to solve problems requiring computations with rational numbers. Furthermore, they should recognize that each rational-number operation will help them solve many different types of problems. Students should be able to estimate a reasonable result for a problem; recall or derive common equivalents for decimals, fractions, and percents; and compute efficiently and accurately with rational numbers. In grades 9–12, students will extend their ability to estimate the results of computations with rational numbers and to understand and judge the reasonableness of numerical results displayed by calculators and computers.

Students' understanding of number lays the foundation for their understanding of algebra, and their fluency with number operations is fundamental to their development of fluency with symbolic operations. The mathematical habits of mind that students bring with them to high school play an equally important role in helping them generalize their understanding of arithmetic to their developing understanding of algebra. Students' work in middle school should assure them that they can grasp the operations of algebra from the conceptualizations, visualizations, and multiple representations of the meanings that they have explored in operations with rational numbers. For example, high school students should be able to see the connections between an algorithm that they develop for multiplying polynomials and the area model for multiplying numbers that they have explored in middle school. Such a connection should also highlight how the distributive property applies to each situation.

Similarly, the multiplicative reasoning skills that students develop in the middle grades should help them develop and extend their understanding of linear functions. The skills that they develop should also prepare them to apply proportional reasoning to diverse mathematical content domains and other fields of study. Finally, middle-grades students' reasoning should expand to include reversibility, flexibility, and the ability to generalize—skills that they will refine in high school mathematics.

As a teacher of mathematics, you face the challenge of providing a learning environment in which students can see, touch, understand, and learn mathematics. Though the challenge is daunting, you must create such an environment to support your students' efforts to understand, re-create, apply, and retain the patterns of mathematics. Students gain mathematical independence when they see their mathematical understanding as something that they can develop and nurture successfully.

The skills, processes, understandings, and mathematical power that you help your students gain in the middle grades are essential. With your guidance, they will cross the bridge, not only to high school, but also to a lifelong understanding of and facility with mathematics.

NAVIGATIONS
SERIES

GRADES 6–8

NAVIGATING *through* NUMBER *and* OPERATIONS

Appendix

Blackline Masters and Solutions

The Fund-Raising Thermometer

Name _____

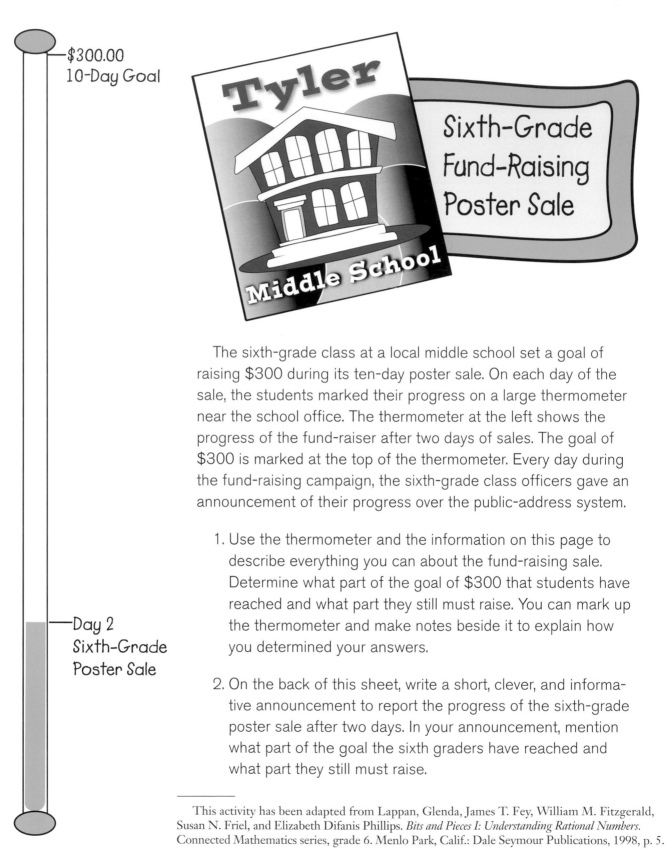

**$300.00
10-Day Goal**

**Day 2
Sixth-Grade
Poster Sale**

The sixth-grade class at a local middle school set a goal of raising $300 during its ten-day poster sale. On each day of the sale, the students marked their progress on a large thermometer near the school office. The thermometer at the left shows the progress of the fund-raiser after two days of sales. The goal of $300 is marked at the top of the thermometer. Every day during the fund-raising campaign, the sixth-grade class officers gave an announcement of their progress over the public-address system.

1. Use the thermometer and the information on this page to describe everything you can about the fund-raising sale. Determine what part of the goal of $300 that students have reached and what part they still must raise. You can mark up the thermometer and make notes beside it to explain how you determined your answers.

2. On the back of this sheet, write a short, clever, and informative announcement to report the progress of the sixth-grade poster sale after two days. In your announcement, mention what part of the goal the sixth graders have reached and what part they still must raise.

This activity has been adapted from Lappan, Glenda, James T. Fey, William M. Fitzgerald, Susan N. Friel, and Elizabeth Difanis Phillips. *Bits and Pieces I: Understanding Rational Numbers.* Connected Mathematics series, grade 6. Menlo Park, Calif.: Dale Seymour Publications, 1998, p. 5.

Science Fair

Name _____

Three middle schools are going to hold a science fair in an auditorium. The amount of space given to each school will be based on the number of students in the school. Bret Harte Middle School has about 1000 students, Malcolm X Middle School has about 600 students, and Kennedy Middle School has about 400 students.

1. Suppose that the rectangle below represents the auditorium.

    a. Divide the rectangle to show the amount of space that each school will get. Label each section "BH" (for Bret Harte), "MX" (for Malcolm X), or "K" (for Kennedy).

    b. Explain your mathematical reasons for dividing the rectangle as you did.

2. What fraction of the space should each school get on the basis of the number of students? Show your mathematical reasoning.

    Bret Harte Middle School _____

    Malcolm X Middle School _____

    Kennedy Middle School _____

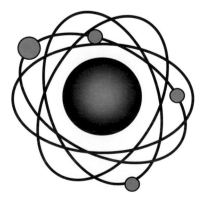

SCIENCE FAIR

Name _____

3. If the schools divide the cost of the science fair according to the number of students at each school, what percentage of the cost will each school pay? Justify your answers.

Bret Harte Middle School _____%

Malcolm X Middle School _____%

Kennedy Middle School _____%

4. If the cost of the science fair is $300, how much will each school pay? Justify your answers.

Bret Harte Middle School _____

Malcolm X Middle School _____

Kennedy Middle School _____

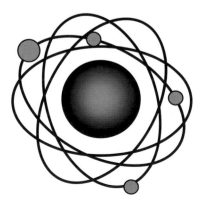

SCIENCE FAIR

A Handy Survey

Name _____

Four students read in a book that 10% of all people are left-handed. This statistic surprised them. They decided to take a small survey to see how their school's percentage compared to the percentage in the book.

Each student visited a different homeroom and asked 20 students whether they were right-handed or left-handed. Here are the results of their survey:

Ms. Grey's Homeroom		**Ms. LaRue's Homeroom**		**Ms. Davison's Homeroom**		**Mr. Fisher's Homeroom**	
Right	19	Right	17	Right	18	Right	17
Left	1	Left	3	Left	2	Left	3
Total	20	Total	20	Total	20	Total	20

1. Did the students' survey produce a higher or lower percentage of left-handed people than the percentage in the book? _____

2. Explain your answer or show how you determined it.

This activity has been adapted from Parke, Carole S., Suzanne Lane, Edward A. Silver, and Maria E. Magone. *Using Assessment to Improve Middle-Grades Mathematics Teaching and Learning: Suggested Activities Using QUASAR Tasks, Scoring Criteria, and Students' Work*. Reston, Va.: NCTM, 2004.

Representing Shaded Areas of Rectangular Grids

Name _____

For each of the rectangular grids below, express the shaded region as a fraction, a decimal, and a percentage of the total area. Explain your reasoning in the space below each grid.

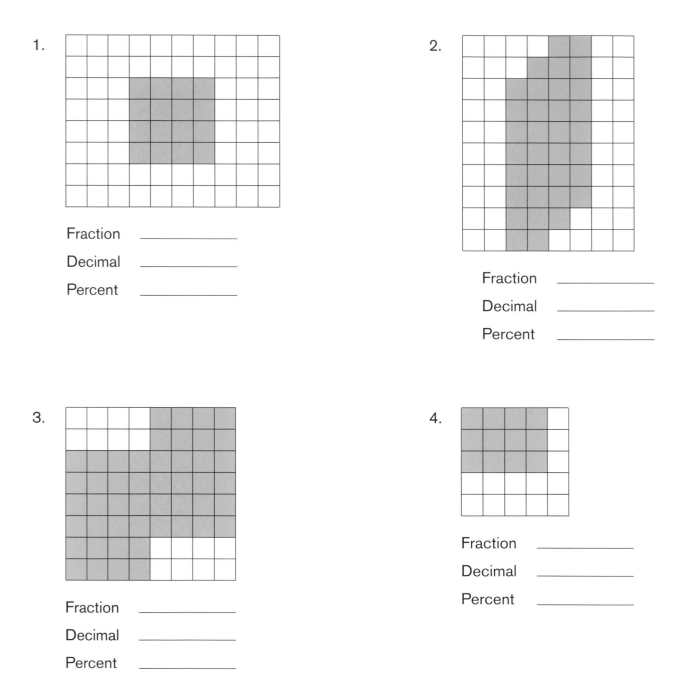

1.

Fraction _____

Decimal _____

Percent _____

2.

Fraction _____

Decimal _____

Percent _____

3.

Fraction _____

Decimal _____

Percent _____

4.

Fraction _____

Decimal _____

Percent _____

This activity has been adapted from Foreman, Linda Cooper, and Albert B. Bennett, Jr. *Visual Mathematics Course II*. Salem, Ore.: Math Learning Center, 1996.

Navigating through Number and Operations in Grades 6–8

Representing Shaded Areas of Rectangular Grids (continued)

Name _____

5.

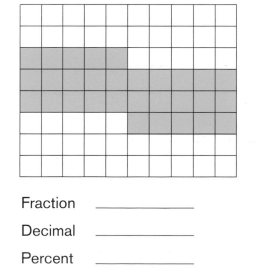

Fraction _____

Decimal _____

Percent _____

6.

Fraction _____

Decimal _____

Percent _____

7.

Fraction _____

Decimal _____

Percent _____

8.

Fraction _____

Decimal _____

Percent _____

Shading Areas of Rectangular Grids

Name _____

Use what you know about fractions, decimals, and percentages to solve the following problems.

1. *a.* Shade the portion of the area of the rectangle that represents 0.725.

   b. What fractional part of the area did you shade?

   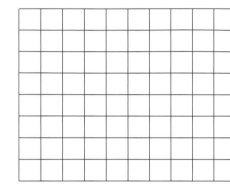

   c. What percentage of the area did you shade?

2. *a.* Shade 3/8 of the area of the rectangle.

   b. What percentage of the area did you shade?

   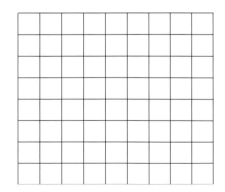

   c. What decimal number does the shaded portion of the rectangle represent?

3. *a.* Shade 87.5% of the area of the rectangle.

   b. What fractional part of the area did you shade?

   c. What decimal number does the shaded portion of the rectangle represent?

This activity has been adapted from Foreman, Linda Cooper, and Albert B. Bennett, Jr. *Visual Mathematics Course II*. Salem, Ore.: Math Learning Center, 1996.

Navigating through Number and Operations in Grades 6–8

Thinking about Mathematical Ideas

Name _____

Your teacher will give you a mathematical idea to write in the blank below. Think about this idea, and answer each of the questions. Use the back of this sheet or another sheet of paper if you need more space. Work by yourself, but be prepared to share your ideas and examples in a group or a class discussion. Use grid paper, cubes, tiles, number strips, or any other resource that your teacher provides to help you with your work.

Mathematical Idea _____

_____

1. How would you explain this mathematical idea?

2. Show what you think this mathematical idea means by drawing one or more diagrams.

3. List three problems that you can use the mathematical idea to solve. One should be easy for you, one should hard for you, and one should be in-between. Label each problem and show your solution and reasoning.

4. Can you think of a problem that uses this idea that you can solve in more than one way? Write the problem and show your solution methods and reasoning.

5. What question(s) do you have about this mathematical idea?

Linden's Algorithm

Name _____

A middle school student named Linden wrote the following entry in her mathematics journal:

Sometimes I think I understand a math topic completely. Then we'll learn about another topic that shows me even more about the topic I thought I knew. Sometimes the new topic even makes me rethink what I know and helps me understand everything better. This is how learning math seems to work.

Linden wrote about the area representation of multiplication as an example of a topic that made her rethink what she knew:

In elementary school, I learned to show simple products of whole numbers as rectangles. I used linear units for the lengths of the edges of the rectangle (the factors) and square units for the area of the rectangle (the product).

Now Linden is learning to multiply fractions, and she wrote that she could apply the area representation to this new situation:

Using the area representation to multiply 5/7 X 6/8 seems to fit right in with what I already know about multiplying 5 X 6. Changing from whole numbers to fractions just means changing area and linear units.

Here is a diagram like the one that Linden drew to show the product 5/7 X 6/8, paired with a diagram like the one that she drew for 5 × 6:

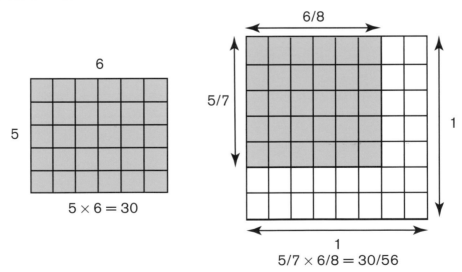

1. Study Linden's statements and the diagrams. What step-by-step procedures do you think Linden used to find the product of 5/7 and 6/8?

Name _____

2. Does Linden's method work for products of other fractions? If so, sketch several examples that show how you can adapt it for the other fractions. If Linden's method does not work, explain why not.

3. Linden extended her entry in her journal:

> *After I solved several multiplication problems with my area method, I noticed a pattern in the computations that I do to get the answers. This pattern helped me invent an algorithm that uses numbers and math symbols. I just imagine the rectangle that represents the problem and then I can 'see' what computations to do.*

Linden went on to explain the computations that she uses to get the product of two fractions.

a. Explain the computational algorithm that you think Linden used and how her computations relate to what she "sees" in the rectangles that she imagines.

b. Show how Linden's computational algorithm would work for the products $5/7 \times 6/8$ and $3/4 \times 4/5$.

Name _____

4. Linden continued in her journal:

I was really surprised—and confused—to see that multiplying two fractions could give an answer that was smaller than the two fractions. In all the work I have done with whole numbers, multiplying always gives an answer that is greater than both of the factors.

 a. How does Linden's area representation of $5/7 \times 6/8$ show that $30/56$ is smaller than both $5/7$ and $6/8$?

 b. Do you think that products of fractions are *always* less than both factors? _____ Explain and show your reasoning, and give examples to illustrate your ideas.

 c. Do you think that products of decimal fractions are always less than both factors? _____ Explain and show your reasoning, and give examples to illustrate your ideas.

Linden's Algorithm Revisited

Name _____

After Linden realized that she could use the area representation model for the multiplication of fractions as well as whole numbers, she began to think about using this model to solve other types of multiplication problems. She wrote in her journal:

> *Finding other products also fits right in with my thinking about the area representation of multiplication. For example, I can also use the area representation to compute 14 X 23, 1.4 X 2.3, and (x + 4)(2x + 3), and I can use the same rectangle for all three problems.*

1. Below are three copies of the rectangle that Linden used. Each one is paired with one of the products that Linden said she could represent. Using numbers, label the diagrams to show how she could find each product. If you don't think you can show the products, explain why (use the back of this sheet sheet if you need more space).

14 × 23

1.4 × 2.3

(x + 4)(2x + 3)

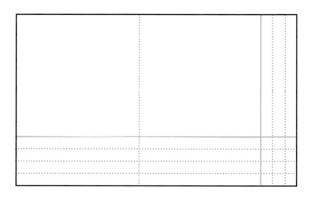

Name _____

2. Consider Linden's representation of the product $\frac{5}{7} \times \frac{6}{7}$ shown below.

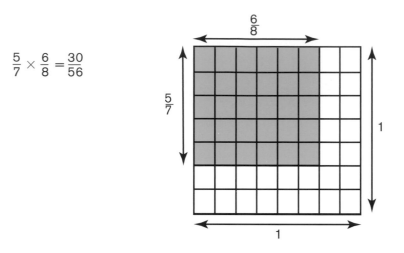

$$\frac{5}{7} \times \frac{6}{8} = \frac{30}{56}$$

How could you adjust Linden's visual method to show the product $2\frac{3}{4} \times 1\frac{4}{5}$? Use the grid below.

3. From the visual representation that you created in question 2, what computational statement can you write?

Erica's Algorithm

Name _____

Erica is a classmate of Linden, whose algorithm for multiplying fractions you have already explored. Like Linden, Erica experimented with area representations for the multiplication of fractions. She wrote in her journal:

Here is how I solve 3/4 x 2/5 visually. I make a rectangle that is 3/4 x 2/5. Then I always enlarge the dimensions of the rectangle to whole numbers, which are easier for me to think about.

1. In step 1, Erica draws an area representation of 3/4 × 2/5. Study the other diagrams, which are like Erica's. What does Erica do in steps 2–4? Explain her reasoning.

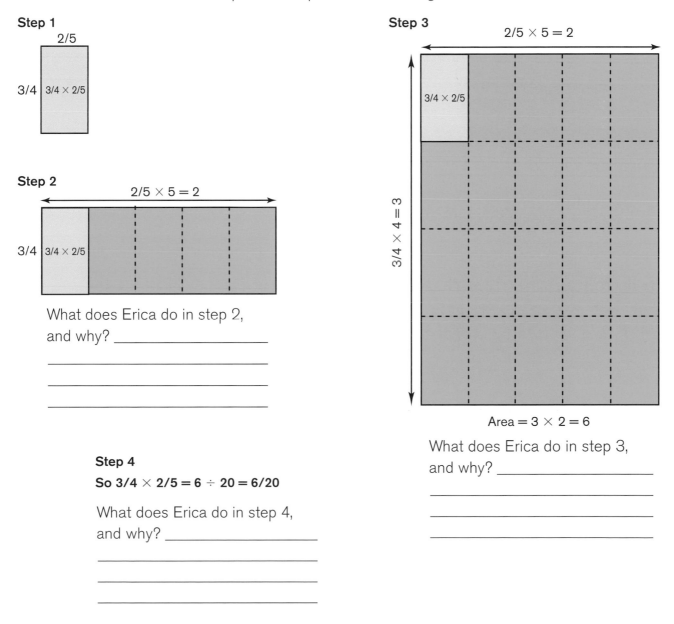

Step 1

2/5

3/4 | 3/4 × 2/5

Step 2

2/5 × 5 = 2

3/4 | 3/4 × 2/5

What does Erica do in step 2,
and why? _____
_____
_____
_____

Step 4

So 3/4 × 2/5 = 6 ÷ 20 = 6/20

What does Erica do in step 4,
and why? _____
_____
_____
_____

Step 3

2/5 × 5 = 2

3/4 × 2/5

3/4 × 4 = 3

Area = 3 × 2 = 6

What does Erica do in step 3,
and why? _____
_____
_____
_____

Name _____

2. Use the back of this sheet to show how Erica's visual method would work for the following products:

   a. 2/3 × 3/7

   b. 3/5 × 1/2

   c. 4/3 × 5/6

3. Write a set of instructions for solving any multiplication of fractions with Erica's visual method.

4. Erica wrote:

   I invented an algorithm that uses the same computations that Linden used, but my reasoning behind why I compute (3 × 2)/(4 × 5) to solve 3/4 × 2/5 is totally different.

   Do you agree? _____ Explain.

5. Will Erica's visual reasoning and computational process work for finding the products of mixed numbers? _____ Of decimals? _____ If so, show how. If not, explain why.

Keonna's Conjecture

Name _____

Keonna is in the same class as Linden and Erica, whose algorithms for the multiplication of fractions you have now examined. Keonna decided to try to use area representations to investigate the division of fractions. She wrote in her journal:

After drawing lots of diagrams, I think that these problems—
9 ÷ 8, 9/10 ÷ 8/10, 9/4 ÷ 8/4, 9/12 ÷ 8/12, and 9/5 ÷ 8/5 — all have
the same answer.

9 ÷ 8 =

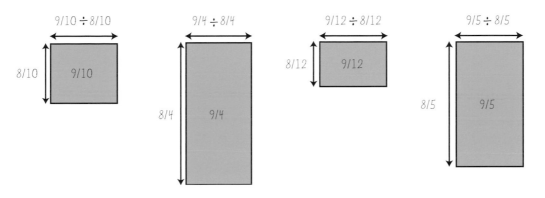

I conjecture that as long as the numerators in the division problem are 9 and 8 and the denominators are equal, the answers will always be the same. But I'm not sure why yet, so I'd like to investigate some more. And I wonder whether this idea will work for other numerators. Also, will it work for addition, subtraction, or multiplication?

On the back of this sheet, or on an additional sheet of paper if necessary, answer the following questions.

1. Use visual representations to show why you think Keonna's conjecture is true or false.

2. Will Keonna's idea work for other numerators? _____ Use diagrams and careful reasoning to support your ideas.

3. Will Keonna's idea work for addition, subtraction, or multiplication? _____ Use diagrams and careful reasoning to support your ideas.

Fraction Situations

Name _____

For each of the following scenarios, sketch a diagram that shows the mathematical relationships in the situation. List several mathematical questions about the situation that you think you can answer by reasoning from your diagram. Then answer your questions and show or explain your reasoning. Use the back of this sheet if necessary.

1. Timberline Track Team

At Timberline Middle School, $\frac{5}{8}$ of the sixth-grade class are girls, and $\frac{2}{3}$ of the sixth-grade girls are on the track team. All the sixth-grade boys are on the track team.

2. Jamaal's Snowstorm

After a heavy January snowstorm, the snow in Jamaal's front yard was 42 inches deep, which is $3\frac{1}{2}$ times as deep as it was before the storm. The amount of new snow that fell during the storm is $\frac{5}{6}$ of the all-time record for a snowstorm in Jamaal's state.

3. City Soccer Fields

The city parks department purchased land for new soccer fields. This rectangular plot of land covers $\frac{3}{4}$ of a square mile and is bordered on one side by a road that is $\frac{2}{3}$ of a mile long. Fencing costs $4400 per $\frac{1}{4}$ of a mile. Grass seed costs $40 per 25-pound bag. Five pounds of grass seed cover $\frac{1}{5}$ of a square mile.

Buying Pizza

Name _____

Answer each of the following questions. Explain your strategy for each one by using diagrams, sketches, or equations.

1. Ms. Carson plans to order pizza for a class party. She thinks that 4 pizzas will be enough for 10 people. Counting students and parent helpers, she needs to order enough pizza for 40 people. How many pizzas should she order? Describe your strategy.

2. The pizzas at Grande's Pizza are really large. Ms. Carson thinks that 4 pizzas will be enough for 16 people. How many pizzas should she order for the 40 people at the class party?

3. At Broadway Pizza, 4 small pizzas are enough for 6 people. At this rate, for how many people will 6 pizzas be enough?

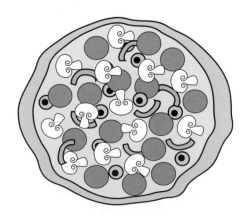

Exchanging Currency

Name _____

When you travel to another country, you must use that country's currency to pay for your hotel, taxis, food, and other purchases. So you have to exchange your money for money used in that country. For example, if you traveled to England, you would exchange your dollars ($) for British pounds (£). The exact exchange rate varies daily.

Imagine that you are planning a trip to London, England. You think a small chart showing the value in pounds for some amounts in dollars will be a helpful guide. Complete the table showing the given amounts of dollars with the corresponding numbers of pounds if the exchange rate is $3 for £2.

Dollars	Pounds
$3.00	
$6.00	
$9.00	
$12.00	
$15.00	
$18.00	

1. Explain how you completed the table.

2. Examine the table. Describe at least three different patterns that you see.

3. How many pounds would you receive in exchange for $150? _____ How many dollars would you receive in exchange for £16? _____

4. Write a rule to help you determine the number of pounds that you will receive in exchange for any given number of dollars. Use *p* for the number of pounds and *d* for the number of dollars.

$ £ $ £ $ £ $ £ $ £

Name _____

5. Change the rule that you wrote in question 4 to help you determine the number of dollars that you will receive in exchange for any given number of pounds. Use *d* for the number of dollars and *p* for the number of pounds.

6. Use the appropriate rule from question 4 or question 5 to answer the following questions.

   a. One adult's ticket for the London Zoo costs £8.50, and one child's ticket costs £6.00. If two adults and one child go to the zoo, how much will the tickets cost in dollars? _____ Explain or show how you arrived at your answer.

   b. Suppose that three tickets to Agatha Christie's play *The Mousetrap* at St. Martin's Theatre in London cost $340. How much will the three tickets cost in pounds? _____ Explain or show how you arrived at your answer.

7. Make a graph for the rule that gives the number of pounds for any number of dollars. Use grid paper, a graphing calculator, or a computer with a spreadsheet software program. Describe what the graph looks like. Look especially at the slope and *y*-intercept.

$ £ $ £ $ £ $ £ $ £

Centimeter Grid Paper

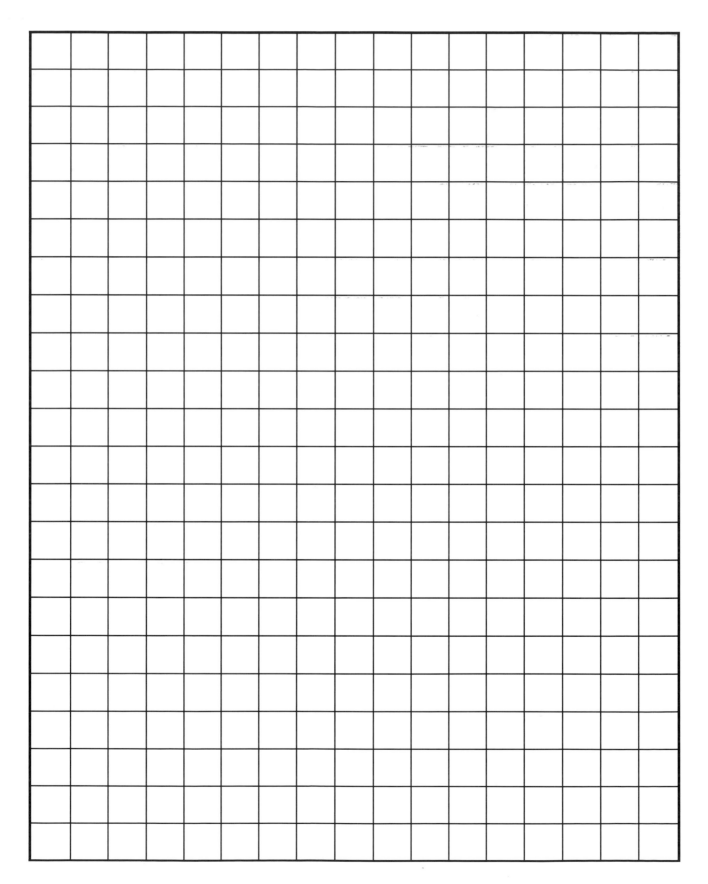

Navigating through Number and Operations in Grades 6–8

Pledge Drive

Name _____

Andrea is riding her bike in a bike-a-thon to raise money for a charity. Each person who participates raises money by asking friends and neighbors to pledge a certain amount of money. Andrea asks each sponsor for a pledge of $1.50 plus $0.50 for every kilometer that she rides on her bike. She decides to make a chart to show people how much money they are pledging for particular numbers of kilometers.

Complete the chart, showing how much money Andrea will raise for each number of kilometers.

1. Explain how you completed the table.

Kilometers	Money Pledged
5	
10	
15	
20	
25	
30	

2. Examine the table. Describe at least three different patterns that you see.

3. *a.* How much money will Andrea receive from each sponsor if she rides 50 kilometers?

_____

b. How many kilometers will she need to ride to receive $22.50 from each sponsor?

_____

Name _____

4. Write a rule to help you determine the amount of money Andrea will raise for any given number of kilometers that she rides on her bike. Use *m* for the amount of money and *k* for the number of kilometers.

5. Change the rule you wrote in question 4 to help you determine the number of kilometers Andrea will need to ride to raise any given amount of money. Use *k* for the number of kilometers and *m* for the amount of money.

6. Use the appropriate rule from question 4 or question 5 to answer the following questions:

   a. Suppose that Andrea received $52.50 from each sponsor. How many kilometers did she ride her bike? _____ Explain or show how you arrived at your answer.

   b. Andrea thinks she can ride her bike 200 kilometers. If she does, how much money will she receive from each sponsor for the charity? _____ Explain or show how you arrived at your answer.

Name _____

7. Make a graph for the rule that gives the number of dollars for any number of kilometers. Use the grid, a graphing calculator, or a computer with a spreadsheet software program. Be sure to label the axes and give your graph a title. In the space below the grid, describe what the graph looks like. Look especially at the slope and *y*-intercept.

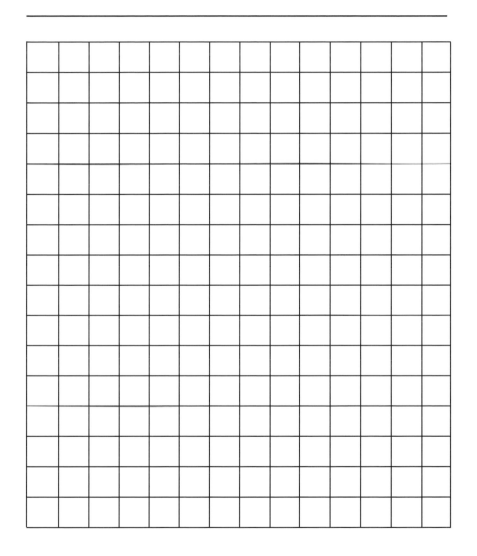

Poring over the Patterns

Name _____

Comparing Tables, Rules, and Graphs—Part 1

Transfer the data from your tables in Exchanging Currency and Pledge Drive to the tables below. Under each table, write the rules that you developed for the relationships between the two quantities in the table.

Exchanging Currency

$ Dollars	£ Pounds

Rules:

Pledge Drive

Kilometers	Money Pledged

Rules:

1. As the number of dollars increases by $3, by how much does the number of British pounds increase? _____

2. As the number of kilometers increases by 5 kilometers, by how much does the amount of money increase? _____

3. If you triple any number of dollars in the Exchanging Currency table, what happens to the number of British pounds? _____ Do you see the same pattern in the Pledge Drive table if you triple any number of kilometers? _____

Name _____

4. Rewrite the data in each table as rates—pounds/dollars and dollars/kilometers. Describe anything special that you observe about these rates.

5. Compare your rate from question 4 for Exchanging Currency (pounds/dollars) with the rules that you listed for the Exchanging Currency table at the beginning of this activity sheet. Describe anything special that you see.

6. Questions 1–5 have helped you compare patterns in the two tables and make connections between those patterns and the rules that you wrote describing the data. Have you noticed any special features for the data in the Exchanging Currency table? Summarize your observations below.

Getting a Grip on the Graphs

Name _____

Comparing Tables, Rules, and Graphs—Part 2

On the following grids, graph the rule $p = (2/3)d$ for the Exchanging Currency table. On the second grid, graph the rule $m = (0.5)k + 1.5$ for the Pledge Drive table. Be sure to label the axes of your graphs.

Exchanging Currency
$$p = (2/3)d$$

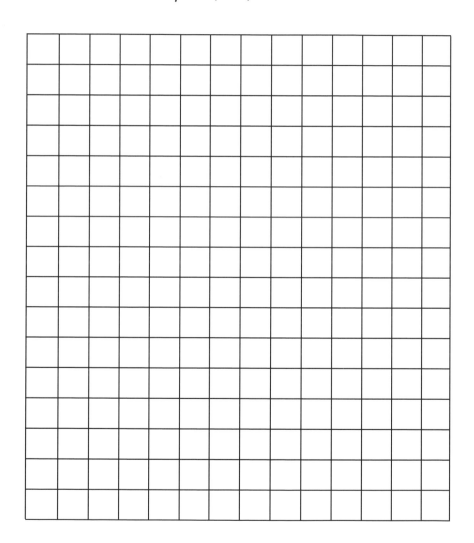

Name _____

Pledge Drive
$$m = (0.5)k + 1.5$$

Describe how the graphs are alike and different.

Name _____

1. *a.* Why does the line for the Exchanging Currency data cross the *y*-axis at the origin and the line for the Pledge Drive data *not* cross the *y*-axis at the origin?

   b. Did you know that the lines would appear that way before you graphed the rules? _____ Explain your thinking.

2. One of these two situations represents a special linear relationship. The relationship between quantities shown in the table for one of these situations is *proportional*. The rule describing the relationship in the proportional situation involves only multiplication or division. Which of these two situations is proportional? _____ Explain your thinking.

3. What are some of the observations that you made for the table, rules, and graph in Exchanging Currency that were not true for the table, rules, and graph in Pledge Drive?

Proposing a Proportional Plan

Name _____

Comparing Tables, Rules, and Graphs—Part 3

Can you change Andrea's system for raising money for a charity (from the activity Pledge Drive) so that Andrea is working with a *proportional* relationship between the amount of money (*m*) that each of her sponsors pledges and the number of kilometers (*k*) that she rides on her bike?

1. Develop a data table, as in Exchanging Currency and Pledge Drive, for a proportional relationship for Andrea, and find one of the rules for your table.

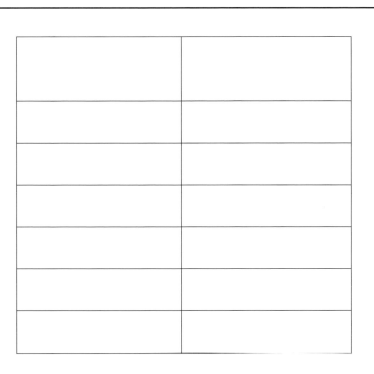

2. Graph your new data on the grid on the next page. Be sure to label the axes and title your graph.

3. Explain why your new system is proportional by describing characteristics of your rule, your graph, and the patterns in your table.

Proposing a Proportional Plan (continued)

Name _____

Grid for step 2

Changing Rates

Name _____

Read each problem. In your group, discuss whether each rate changes, and if so, how. Once you have discussed all the problems, cut them out from one set of activity pages and sort them into these categories: **Rate Increases, Rate Decreases, Rate Stays the Same,** and **Cannot Tell.** Your teacher has given you a sheet of paper on which to tape the problems to display them in the appropriate categories. Look at your display. What generalizations can you make about changes in the two quantities that make up a rate? For example, what changes always reduce a rate? Discuss your ideas in your group, and be ready to explain them to the class.

Problem 1

Josie noticed that the cost of bags of candy at the wholesale club changed from last week. Today she paid more money for fewer bags of candy. How did the cost per bag change?

Problem 2

The London Bank gave more British pounds in exchange for the same number of U.S. dollars this week than it did last week. Did the exchange rate, £/$, increase, decrease, or stay the same—or can't you tell?

Problem 3

Marta rides her bike every morning. She keeps track of the distance and time that she rides. Today she traveled a greater distance and rode a longer time than she did yesterday. How did her speed change?

Problem 4

Rodrigo has a recipe for making lemonade. He mixes some lemonade concentrate with some water. He decides to change the recipe, decreasing the amount of lemonade concentrate and increasing the amount of water. Does the lemonade taste stronger, weaker, or the same—or can't you tell?

Name _____

Problem 5

Today the London Bank gave fewer British pounds in exchange for fewer U.S. dollars than it did yesterday. Did the exchange rate, £/$, increase, decrease, or stay the same—or can't you tell?

Problem 6

Thomas rode his bike the same distance today as yesterday, but today he took a longer time. Did his speed increase, decrease, or stay the same—or can't you tell?

Problem 7

Rodrigo changed his lemonade mixture again. This time he kept the amount of lemonade concentrate the same as in his new recipe in problem 4 but decreased the amount of water. What happened to the taste of his new lemonade compared with the taste of the lemonade he created in problem 4? Did the new lemonade taste stronger, weaker, or the same—or can't you tell?

Problem 8

Josie paid less money today than she did yesterday for the same number of bags of candy. How did the cost per bag change?

Using a Unit Rate to Solve Problems

Name _____

1. Marcus runs around the track every day after school. He believes that with practice he can be a track star. He can run 12 laps around the school's track in 30 minutes.

   a. What are the two possible rates for this situation?

   b. Rewrite each rate as a unit rate.

   c. What does each unit rate tell you?

   d. Suppose someone asks you, "At this rate, how long will it take Marcus to run 14 laps?" Which unit rate will you use to answer the question? _____ Explain why you chose that unit rate, and then use it to answer the question.

   e. Suppose someone then asks, "At this rate, how many laps can Marcus run in 5 minutes?" Which unit rate will you use to answer the question? _____ Explain why you chose that unit rate, and then use it to answer the question.

Name _____

2. Michelle, an exchange student from France, will be in the United States for the next four months. In France, she buys everything in euros. When she came to the United States, she had to exchange her euros for U.S. dollars. She went to the bank and exchanged her money at the rate of 4.5 euros for 5 dollars.

a. What are the two possible rates for this situation?

b. Rewrite each rate as a unit rate.

c. What does each unit rate tell you?

d. Suppose someone asks you, "At this rate, how many euros will Michelle receive for $500?" Which unit rate will you use to answer the question? _____ Explain why you chose that unit rate, and then use it to answer the question.

e. Suppose someone then asks, "At this rate, how many dollars did Michelle receive for 135 euros?" Which unit rate will you use to answer the question? _____ Explain why you chose that unit rate, and then use it to answer the question.

Name _____

3. The Martinez family is planning to drive from New York to Florida during winter break to visit the Kennedy Space Center. The scale on the map that they are using to plan their trip is 2.5 cm = 125 miles.

    a. What are the two possible rates for this situation?

    b. Rewrite each rate as a unit rate.

    c. What docs each unit rate tell you?

    d. Write two questions that you can use a unit rate to answer about the Martinez family's trip to Florida. Use a different unit rate for each question. Answer both your questions, and explain which unit rate you used to find the answer.

Solutions for the Blackline Masters

Solutions for "The Fund-Raising Thermometer"

The students' announcements will vary, but all should mention that the students have reached 1/4 of the goal ($75) and that 3/4 of the goal ($225) remains.

Solutions for "Science Fair"

1. *a.* Configurations will vary; one possible diagram of an allocation of space follows:

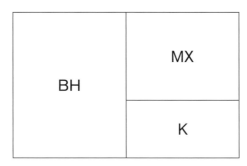

   b. Students' explanations will vary.

2. Bret Harte: 1/2
   Malcolm X: 3/10
   Kennedy: 1/5

3. Bret Harte: 50%
   Malcolm X: 30%
   Kennedy: 20%

4. Bret Harte: $150
   Malcolm X: $90
   Kennedy: $60

Solutions for "A Handy Survey"

1. The students' survey produced a higher percentage of left-handed people than the percentage in the book.

2. The students' explanations will vary. A sample follows: "I changed the ratio of the number of left-handed people surveyed to a percent; 9/80 = 11.25%."

Solutions for "Representing Shaded Areas of Rectangular Grids"

1. 1/5, 0.2, 20%
2. 17/40, 0.425, 42.5%
3. 3/4, 0.75, 75%
4. 12/25, 0.48, 48%
5. 23/50, 0.46, 46%
6. 1/4, 0.25, 25%
7. 3/8, 0.375, 37.5%
8. 27/50, 0.54, 54%

Solutions for "Shading Areas of Rectangular Grids"

1. *a.* The students' choices of areas to shade will vary, but they should cover 58/80 of the rectangle. The diagram shows one example.

   b. 29/40 of the area is shaded.

   c. 72.5% of the area is shaded.

2. *a.* The students' choices of areas to shade will vary, but they should cover 36/96 of the rectangle. The diagram shows one example.

   b. 37.5% of the area is shaded.

   c. 0.375 of the area is shaded.

3. *a.* The students' choices of areas to shade will vary, but they should cover 63/72 of the rectangle. The diagram shows one example.

   b. 7/8 of the area is shaded.

   c. 0.875 of the area is shaded.

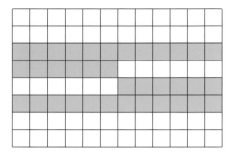

Solutions for "Thinking about Mathematical Ideas"

Mathematical Idea—Addition of whole numbers, fractions, and decimals.

1. Answers will vary; for example, students might explain addition as the joining of two sets of numbers or two parts composing a set of numbers.

2. Answers will vary; two examples of diagrams follow:

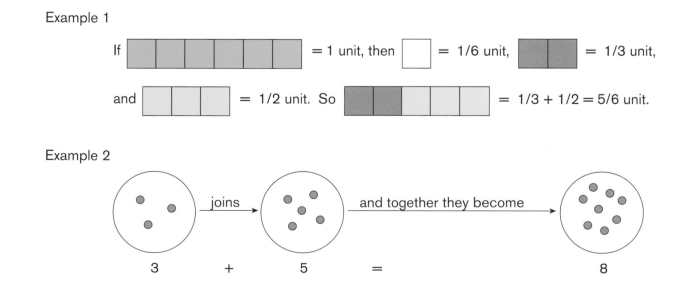

3–5. Answers will vary. For an extended discussion of types of student thinking, see the section "The Meanings of Addition, Multiplication, Subtraction, and Division" in chapter 2 (pp. 37–42).

Solutions for "Linden's Algorithm"

1. Answers will vary. A student's response might be something like, "I think Linden made a 7 × 8 grid and then filled in a 5 × 6 rectangle in the top left corner. So the product 5/7 × 6/8 equals 30/56."

2. Yes, Linden's method does work for products of other fractions. The students' examples will vary, but their problems involving proper fractions will look very similar to Linden's example. Problems involving improper fractions will extend this approach, as shown in the solution for problem 2 on the activity sheet "Linden's Algorithm Revisited."

3. *a.* Answers will vary. One example of how a student might explain Linden's computational algorithm follows: "Linden might say that the product will always be the product of the numerators divided by the product of the denominators. With proper fractions, the computation involves seeing the little rectangle set in the big rectangle."

   b. $(5 \times 7)/(6 \times 8) = 35/48$; $(3 \times 4)/(4 \times 5) = 12/20$.

4. *a.* Answers will vary. One example of a possible response follows: "Linden's representation shows that the product fits in the corner of the diagram. The rectangle represented by the product is part of the rectangle representing 5/7. It is also part of the rectangle representing 6/8."

   b. Examples will vary, but students should agree that for proper fractions, the product is always less than both factors.

   c. Examples will vary, but students should agree that for decimal fractions between 0 and 1, the product is always less than both factors. Their reasoning might be along the following line: "Decimal fractions are just like the other fractions, only with denominators that are multiples of 10."

Solutions for "Linden's Algorithm Revisited"

1. See figure 2.13 (p. 51) for appropriate number labels.

2.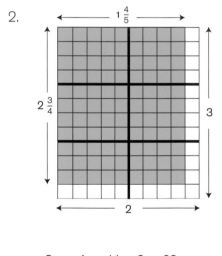

3. $2\dfrac{3}{4} \times 1\dfrac{4}{5} = \dfrac{11}{4} \times \dfrac{9}{5} = \dfrac{99}{20}.$

Solutions for "Erica's Algorithm"

1. Students' answers will vary. Their descriptions might be something like the following: "In step 2 and 3, Erica enlarged the rectangle's dimensions by multiplying by 5 and 4. Then she found the area of the new rectangle. In step 4, to find the area of the original rectangle, Erica divided the area of the new rectangle by the amount she multiplied by to get whole numbers (5 × 4)."

2. a. 2/3 × 3/7

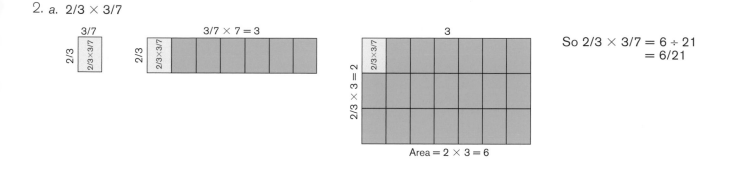

So 2/3 × 3/7 = 6 ÷ 21
                        = 6/21

b. 3/5 × 1/2

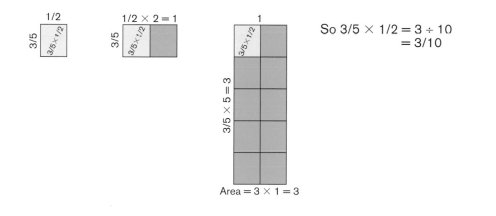

So 3/5 × 1/2 = 3 ÷ 10
                        = 3/10

c. 4/3 × 5/6

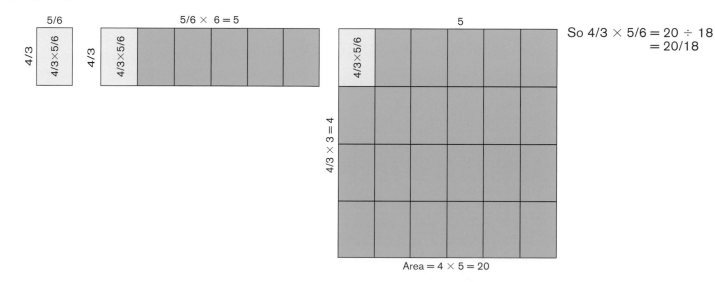

So 4/3 × 5/6 = 20 ÷ 18
                        = 20/18

3. Answers will vary; however, the students' instructions should be some variation on the following: "To use Erica's visual method, enlarge the dimensions of the rectangle to whole numbers. (1) Enlarge the length by enlarging it the number of times in its denominator. (2) Enlarge the width by enlarging it the number of times in its denominator. (3) Find the area of the enlarged rectangle—that is, the product of the numerators. (4) To find the product of the fractions, 'undo' the enlargement by dividing by the product of the amounts by which the figures were enlarged—that is, the product of the denominators."

4. Answers will vary but should focus on the reasoning behind Linden's and Erica's processes rather than the similarity of the solutions.

5. Yes, the method will work for mixed numbers and decimals. Students' explanations will vary.

Solutions for "Keonna's Conjecture"

1. Students should decide that Keonna's conjecture is true, but their representations will vary. Sample solutions appear in the activity's "Discussion" section (pp. 61–63).

2. Yes, Keonna's idea will work for other numerators. See the sample diagrams in the "Discussion" section.

3. No, the conjecture will not hold for addition, subtraction, or multiplication. Students' diagrams and reasoning will vary. The circles at the right illustrate that the conjecture does not work for addition: These circles make it possible to visualize the sum of 1/2 and 1/3. If each denominator is doubled, the total area of the circles will clearly be decreased. Similar arguments can be made for subtraction and multiplication. The conjecture holds only for division.

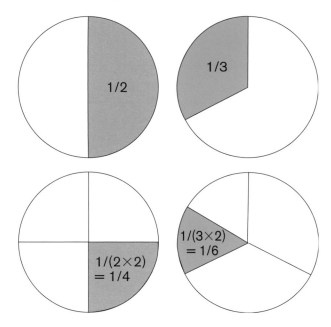

Solutions for "Fraction Situations"

1–3. Questions and answers will vary. Sample solutions appear in the activity's "Discussion" section (pp. 64–69).

Solutions for "Buying Pizza"

1. Assuming that on average a parent helper will eat the same amount of pizza as a student, Ms. Carson should order 16 pizzas for 40 people.

2. Ms. Carson should order 10 pizzas for 40 people at the class party.

3. Six small pizzas from Broadway Pizza will be enough for 9 people.

See the text (pp. 85–88) for further discussion of these solutions.

Solutions for "Exchanging Currency"

1. Students' explanations of how they completed the table (at the right) will vary; a student might say something like, "Since the dollars were increasing by 3, I increased the pounds by 2."

2. Students will identify a variety of patterns; for example, $d/p = 3/2$, $d = (3/2)p$, $p = (2/3)d$ (p = number of British pounds; d = number of dollars).

3. Students would receive £100 in exchange for $150, and $24 in exchange for £16.

4. $p = (2/3)d$ (p = number of British pounds; d = number of dollars).

5. $d = (3/2)p$ (p = number of British pounds; d = number of dollars).

6. *a.* Two adult tickets and one child's ticket will cost £23. If p = £23, then d = $34.50.

   b. If d = $340, then p = £226.66.

7. The graph of the line (shown at right) crosses the *y*-axis (number of pounds) at the origin, with a slope of 2/3, the ratio of pounds to dollars.

Dollars	Pounds
$3.00	£2.00
$6.00	£4.00
$9.00	£6.00
$12.00	£8.00
$15.00	£10.00
$18.00	£12.00

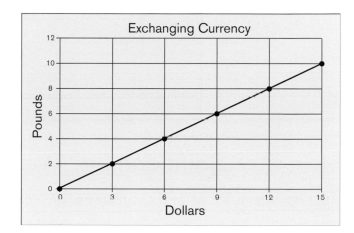

Solutions for "Pledge Drive"

1. Students' explanations of how they completed the table (at the right) will vary.

2. Students will identify a variety of patterns.

3. *a.* If Andrea rides 50 kilometers, she will receive $26.50 from each sponsor.

   b. To receive $22.50 from each sponsor, Andrea will need to ride 42 kilometers.

4. $m = (0.5)k + 1.5$ (k = number of kilometers; m = amount of money).

5. $k = (m - 1.5)/0.5$ (k = number of kilometers; m = amount of money).

Kilometers	Money Pledged
5	$4.00
10	$6.50
15	$9.00
20	$11.50
25	$14.00
30	$16.50

6. *a.* If Andrea received $52.50 from each sponsor, she rode 102 kilometers. Students' explanations will vary.
   b. If Andrea succeeds in riding 200 kilometers, she will receive $101.50 from each sponsor.

7. The graph of the line shown below crosses the *y*-axis (number of dollars) at *m* = 1.5, with a slope of 1/2.

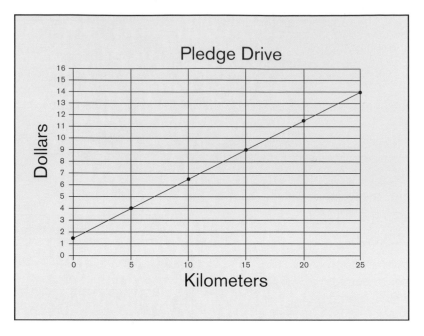

Solutions for "Poring over the Patterns"

Comparing Tables, Rules and Graphs—Part 1

1. As the number of dollars increases by 3, the number of pounds increases by 2.

2. As the number of kilometers increases by 5, the amount of money increases by $2.50.

3. The number of pounds in the Exchanging Currency table triples if the number of dollars triples; this pattern does not hold in the Pledge Drive table if the number of kilometers triples.

4. The rates from the Exchanging Currency table are 2/3, 4/6, 6/9, and so forth, which all equal 2/3; for the Pledge Drive table, the rates are 4/5, 6.5/10, 9/15, and so on, which are not equivalent.

5. The constant rate is the factor in one of the rules for the situation in Exchanging Currency; its reciprocal is the factor in the other rule for the situation.

6. Answers will vary. The students are asked to summarize their observations about connections between the patterns and the rules. The students' summaries should show that they understand what they have been doing, as well as what they have learned from it.

Solutions for "Getting a Grip on the Graphs"

Comparing Tables, Rules and Graphs—Part 2

Both graphs are linear with a positive slope. The graph for Exchanging Currency crosses the *y*-axis at the origin; the graph for Pledge Drive crosses the *y*-axis at 1.5.

1. *a.* The graph of the Exchanging Currency data crosses the *y*-axis at the origin because the rule is defined only by multiplication; unlike the situation in Pledge Drive, the situation in Exchanging Currency does not involve any addition or subtraction.

   b. Answers will vary.

2. The situation in Exchanging Currency is proportional. Students' explanations will vary.

3. Students answers might include the following observations about the table, rules, and graph in Exchanging Currency that are not true of the table, rules, and graph in Pledge Drive:

- If we double the number of dollars, the number of pounds doubles; if we triple the number of dollars, the number of pounds triples, and so on.

- The rates (pounds/dollars) for the data, 2/3, 4/6, 6/9, and so on, are all equivalent (to 2/3).

- The reciprocal rates (dollars/pounds) are all equal (to 3/2).

- The two formulas for the situation are $p = (2/3)d$ and $d = (3/2)p$, where d represents the number of dollars and p represents the number of British pounds. The factors defining the relationships between pounds and dollars (2/3 and 3/2) are the constant rates found in the table.

Solutions for "Proposing a Proportional Plan"

Comparing Tables, Rules and Graphs—Part 3

1–3. Answers will vary, but Andrea's new system must be defined only through multiplication or division. See the discussion of the activity in the text (pp. 97–98) and also inspect figure 3.13 for an example.

Solutions for "Changing Rates"

The following chart summarizes how changes in the numerator and denominator for each problem change the rate. *Problem* appears in capital letters if the rate increases, in lowercase letters if the rate decreases, and in green if it is not possible to tell.

Numerator / Denominator	—	↑	↓
—	None	PROBLEM 2	problem 8
↑	problem 6	problem 3	problem 4
↓	PROBLEM 7	PROBLEM 1	problem 5

Solutions for "Using a Unit Rate to Solve Problems"

1. *a.* Two possible rates for the situation are 12 laps/30 minutes and 30 minutes/12 laps.

   b. As unit rates, these are 0.4 lap/1 minute and 2.5 minutes/1 lap.

   c. The first rate tells how many laps Marcus can run in one minute; the second rate tells how long it takes Marcus to run one lap.

   d. To find how long it will take Marcus to run 14 laps, the students can determine how long it takes Marcus to run 1 lap. Then they can multiply this unit rate, 2.5 minutes/1 lap, by 14 laps. Marcus runs 14 laps in 35 minutes.

   e. To find out how many laps Marcus can run in 5 minutes, the students can determine how many laps Marcus can run in 1 minute. Then they can multiply this unit rate, 0.4 lap/1 minute, by 5 minutes. Marcus runs 2 laps in 5 minutes.

2. *a.* The two possible rates for the situation are 5 dollars/4.5 euros and 4.5 euros/5 dollars.

   b. As unit rates, these are 1.11 dollars/1 euro and 0.9 euros/1 dollar.

c. The first rate tells the number of dollars that equal 1 euro; the second rate tells the fraction of euros that equals $1.

d. To find the number of euros for $500, the students can determine the number of euros for 1 dollar. Then they can multiply this unit rate, 0.9 euros/1 dollar, by 500 dollars. Michelle will receive 450 euros for 500 dollars.

e. To find the number of dollars for 135 euros, the students can determine the number of dollars for one euro. Then they can multiply this unit rate, 1.11 dollars/1 euro, by 135 euros. Michelle will receive 149.85 dollars for 135 euros. Note that the unit rate 1.11 dollars/1 euro is an approximation, rounding down from $1.1\overline{1}$ dollars/1 euro ($5 \div 4.5 = 1.1\overline{1}$). If the students divided 135 euros by the other unit rate, 0.9 euros/1 dollar, they would calculate that Michelle would receive an even 150 dollars in exchange for 135 euros.

3. *a.* The two possible rates are 2.5 cm/25 miles and 25 miles/2.5 cm.

b. As unit rates, these are 0.1 cm/1 mile and 10 miles/1 cm.

c. The first rate tells the number of centimeters that correspond to an actual distance of 1 mile; the second rate tells the number of miles represented by 1 centimeter on the map.

d. Students' answers will vary. Two sample questions follow:
"If the distance on the map is 5 centimeters, how many miles will the family travel?"
"If the family travels 600 miles, how many centimeters on the map did they cover?"

References

Battista, Michael T. "A Complete Model for Operations on Integers." *Arithmetic Teacher* 30 (May 1983): 26–31.

Billings, Esther M. H. "Problems That Encourage Proportion Sense." *Mathematics Teaching in the Middle School* 7 (September 2001): 10–14.

Bright, George W., Wallece Brewer, Kay McClain, and Edward S. Mooney. *Navigating through Data Analysis in Grades 6–8. Principles and Standards for School Mathematics* Navigations Series. Reston, Va.: National Council of Teachers of Mathematics, 2003.

Bright, George W., and John G. Harvey. "Using Games to Teach Fraction Concepts and Skills." In *Mathematics for the Middle Grades (5–9)*, 1982 Yearbook of the National Council of Teachers of Mathematics (NCTM), edited by Linda Silvey, pp. 205–16. Reston, Va.: NCTM, 1982.

Bright, George W., Patricia Lamphere Jordan, Carol Malloy, and Tad Watanabe. *Navigating through Measurement in Grades 6–8. Principles and Standards for School Mathematics* Navigations Series. Reston, Va.: National Council of Teachers of Mathematics, 2005.

Carpenter, Thomas P., Elizabeth Fennema, Megan Loef Franke, Linda Levi, and Susan B. Empson. *Children's Mathematics: Cognitively Guided Instruction.* Portsmouth, N.H., and Reston, Va.: Heinemann and National Council of Teachers of Mathematics, 1999.

Chappell, Michaele F., and Denisse R. Thompson. "Modifying Our Questions to Assess Students' Thinking." *Mathematics Teaching in the Middle School* 4 (April 1999): 470–74.

Cramer, Kathleen, and Thomas Post. "Connecting Research to Teaching: Proportional Reasoning." *Mathematics Teacher* 86 (May 1993): 404–7.

Cramer, Kathleen, Thomas Post, and Sarah Currier. "Learning and Teaching Ratio and Proportion: Research Implications." In *Research Ideas for the Classroom: Middle Grades Mathematics*, National Council of Teachers of Mathematics Research Interpretation Project, edited by Douglas T. Owens, pp. 159–78. New York: Macmillan Publishing Co., 1993.

Fennell, Francis (Skip), and Tom Rowan. "Representation: An Important Process for Teaching and Learning Mathematics." *Teaching Children Mathematics* 7 (January 2001): 288–92.

Foreman, Linda Cooper, and Albert B. Bennett, Jr. *Visual Mathematics Course II.* Salem, Ore.: Math Learning Center, 1996.

Friel, Susan, Sid Rachlin, and Dot Doyle, with the assistance of Claire Nygard, David Pugalee, and Mark Ellis. *Navigating through Algebra in Grades 6–8. Principles and Standards for School Mathematics* Navigations Series. Reston, Va.: National Council of Teachers of Mathematics, 2001.

Heller, Patricia, Thomas R. Post, Merlyn Behr, and Richard Lesh. "Qualitative and Numerical Reasoning about Fractions and Rates by Seventh- and Eighth-Grade Students." *Journal for Research in Mathematics Education* 21 (November 1990): 388–402.

Karplus, Robert, Steven Pulos, and Elizabeth K. Stage. "Proportional Reasoning of Early Adolescents." In *Acquisition of Mathematics Concepts and Processes*, edited by Richard A. Lesh and Marsha Landau, pp. 45–91. New York: Academic Press, 1983.

Kilpatrick, Jeremy, Jane Swafford, and Bradford Findell, eds. *Adding It Up: Helping Children Learn Mathematics.* Washington, D.C.: National Academy Press, 2001.

Lamon, Susan J. "Presenting and Representing: From Fractions to Rational Numbers." In *The Role of Representation in School Mathematics*, 2001 Yearbook of the National Council of Teachers of Mathematics (NCTM), edited by Albert A. Cuoco, pp. 146–65. Reston, Va.: NCTM, 2001.

———. *Teaching Fractions and Ratios for Understanding: Essential Content Knowledge and Instructional Strategies for Teachers*. Hillsdale, N.J.: Lawrence Erlbaum Associates, 1999.

Langrall, Cynthia W., and Jane Swafford. "Three Balloons for Two Dollars: Developing Proportional Reasoning." *Mathematics Teaching in the Middle School* 6 (December 2000): 254–61.

Lappan, Glenda, and Mary K. Bouck. "Developing Algorithms for Adding and Subtracting Fractions." In *The Teaching and Learning of Algorithms in School Mathematics*, 1998 Yearbook of the National Council of Teachers of Mathematics (NCTM), edited by Lorna J. Morrow, pp. 183–97. Reston, Va.: NCTM, 1998.

Lappan, Glenda, James T. Fey, William M. Fitzgerald, Susan N. Friel, and Elizabeth Difanis Phillips. *Bits and Pieces I: Understanding Rational Numbers*. Connected Mathematics series, grade 6. Menlo Park, Calif.: Dale Seymour Publications, 1998.

Miller, Jane Lincoln, and James T. Fey. "Proportional Reasoning." *Mathematics Teaching in the Middle School* 5 (January 2000): 310–13.

National Council of Teachers of Mathematics (NCTM). *Classroom Activities for "Making Sense of Fractions, Ratios, and Proportions,"* companion booklet to the 2002 Yearbook of the National Council of Teachers of Mathematics, edited by George Bright and Bonnie Litwiller. Reston, Va.: NCTM, 2002a.

_____. *Making Sense of Fractions, Ratios, and Proportions*. 2002 Yearbook of the National Council of Teachers of Mathematics, edited by Bonnie Litwiller. Reston, Va.: NCTM, 2002b.

———. *Principles and Standards for School Mathematics*. Reston, Va.: NCTM, 2000.

_____. *Professional Standards for Teaching Mathematics*. Reston, Va.: NCTM, 1991.

_____. "Proportional Reasoning" Focus Issue. *Mathematics Teaching in the Middle School* 8 (April 2003).

Noelting, Gerald. "The Development of Proportional Reasoning and the Ratio Concept: Part I. The Differentiation of Stages." *Educational Studies in Mathematics* 11 (1980): 217–53.

Parke, Carole S., Suzanne Lane, Edward A. Silver, and Maria E. Magone. *Using Assessment to Improve Middle-Grades Mathematics Teaching and Learning: Suggested Activities Using QUASAR Tasks, Scoring Criteria, and Students' Work*. Reston, Va.: NCTM, 2004.

Post, Thomas R., Merlyn J. Behr, and Richard Lesh. "Proportionality and the Development of Prealgebra Understandings." In *The Ideas of Algebra, K–12*, 1988 Yearbook of the National Council of Teachers of Mathematics (NCTM), edited by Arthur F. Coxford, pp. 78–90. Reston, Va.: NCTM, 1988.

Rachlin, Sid. "Learning to See the Wind." *Mathematics Teaching in the Middle School* 3 (May 1998): 470–73.

Rachlin, Sidney L., and Ronald V. Preston. *Algebraic Concepts and Relationships*. Greenville, N.C.: East Carolina University, 2001. Available on the Web at www.cofed.ecu.edu/mathscience/middlemath/curriculum.

Reys, Barbara J. "Teaching Computational Estimation: Concepts and Strategies." In *Estimation and Mental Computation*, 1986 Yearbook of the National Council of Teachers of Mathematics (NCTM), edited by Harold L. Schoen, pp. 31–44. Reston, Va.: NCTM, 1986.

Reys, Robert E. "Computation versus Number Sense." *Mathematics Teaching in the Middle School* 4 (October 1998): 110–12.

Sinicrope, Rose, Harold W. Mick, and John R. Kolb. "Interpretations of Fraction Division." In *Making Sense of Fractions, Ratios, and Proportions*, 2002 Yearbook of the National Council of Teachers of Mathematics (NCTM), edited by Bonnie Litwiller, pp. 153–61. Reston, Va.: NCTM, 2002.

Smith, Margaret Schwan, Edward A. Silver, Mary Kay Stein, Melissa Boston, Marjorie A. Henningsen, and Amy F. Hillen. *Improving Instruction in Rational Numbers and Proportionality: Using Cases to Transform Mathematics Teaching and Learning*, vol. 1. New York: Teachers College Press, 2005.

Smith, Margaret Schwan, and Mary Kay Stein. "Selecting and Creating Mathematical Tasks: From Research to Practice." *Mathematics Teaching in the Middle School* 3 (February 1998): 344–50.

Stein, Mary Kay, and Suzanne Lane. "Instructional Tasks and the Development of Student Capacity to Think and Reason: An Analysis of the Relationship between Teaching and Learning in a Reform Mathematics Project." *Educational Research and Evaluation* 2 (October 1996): 50–80.

Stein, Mary Kay, and Margaret Schwan Smith. "Mathematical Tasks as a Framework for Reflection: From Research to Practice." *Mathematics Teaching in the Middle School* 3 (January 1998): 268–75.

Thompson, Charles S., and William S. Bush. "Improving Middle School Teachers' Reasoning about Proportional Reasoning." *Mathematics Teaching in the Middle School* 8 (April 2003): 398–403.

Turner, Julianne C., Karen Rossman Styers, and Debra G. Daggs. "Encouraging Mathematical Thinking." *Mathematics Teaching in the Middle School* 3 (September 1997): 66–72.

Vergnaud, Gerard. "Multiplicative Structures." In *Acquisition of Mathematics Concepts and Processes*, edited by Richard A. Lesh and Marsha Landau, pp. 128–75. New York: Academic Press, 1983.

Warrington, Mary Ann. "How Children Think about Division with Fractions." *Mathematics Teaching in the Middle School* 2 (May 1997): 390–95.

Wearne, Diana, and Vicky L. Kouba. "Rational Numbers." In *Results from the Seventh Mathematics Assessment of the National Assessment of Educational Progress*, edited by Edward A. Silver and Patricia Ann Kenney, pp. 163–91. Reston, Va.: National Council of Teachers of Mathematics, 2000.